GW00535772

“SOMEWHERE IN THE WEST COUNTRY”

Other Crécy titles by Ken Wakefield

THE FIRST PATHFINDERS
OPERATION BOLERO
PFADFINDER: GERMAN PATHFINDERS OVER BRITAIN, 1940–44
(*Autumn 1997*)

"SOMEWHERE IN THE WEST COUNTRY"

The History of Bristol (Whitchurch) Airport, 1930–1957

Ken Wakefield

CRÉCY

Published in 1997 by
Crécy Publishing Limited,
Southside, Manchester Airport, Wilmslow,
Cheshire SK9 4LL, United Kingdom

ISBN 0 947554 65 3

Typeset in Monotype Baskerville by
Ace Filmsetting Ltd, Frome, Somerset

Printed and bound in Great Britain by
Creative Print & Design

Contents

Acknowledgements

While some of this book is based on personal recollections and notes, much of it was derived from information published in aviation magazines, newspapers and other publications of the 1929–1957 period. Among these were 'The Aeroplane', 'Flight', 'Wessex Airways' (the newsletter of the Bristol and Wessex Aeroplane Club in the 1930s), 'BOAC Review and News Letter', and the Bristol Evening World and Evening Post. Further useful details were gleaned from brochures, programmes and booklets produced by the Corporation of Bristol and the pre-war Bristol Development Board.

Information also came from a number of aviation enthusiasts and I am grateful to them all. In particular my thanks go to Tony Pitchers, who also supplied many photographs. Others who made valuable contributions were Ian James, Bernard Morey, David Leech, Andy Hartles, Tom Turner and the late Richard Ashley Hall.

Many of the photos in this book originated from Ken Kilsby and Pat Dobbs, but much to my regret neither of these good friends lived to see this history in print. Ken was a Whitchurch devotee whose photographic activities covered the entire life-span of the airport, while Pat's aviation interests encompassed events in and around Weston-super-Mare as well as Bristol. Other photos were kindly supplied by the late A J Jackson, Mac Hawkins (through whom I obtained numerous photos taken at Whitchurch by the late Ivo Peters), Don Loader, Mike Tozer, the late Reece Winstone, BOAC/British Airways (including some via Adrian Meredith Studios), the Imperial War Museum, the Evening World, the Welsh Industrial and Maritime Museum, and other sources as credited. Although the quality of some photos is not good, they have been included for their historical interest. The origins of others are obscure, having come from various private collections, but every effort has been made to establish their true copyright. However, this has not always been possible, and apologies are tendered in advance for any incorrect credits.

Ken Wakefield
June 1997

Introduction

I first became aware of Bristol (Whitchurch) Airport in the summer of 1933, when I was four years old. My family had recently moved to live on the southern outskirts of the city, and one day my father, sister and I set out to explore the adjacent countryside. Tired from walking in the hot sun, we sat down beside a haystack, and shortly afterwards a small aeroplane came into sight, its engine quietly ticking over as it came in to land in a nearby field. In those days it was quite an event to see an aeroplane in flight, and as we set off to look for its landing place I could scarcely believe that I might actually see one on the ground. We soon came to a very large field and there in the far corner was a never to be forgotten sight – it was, I was told by my father, 'a biplane', and the field was called 'Whitchurch Airport'.

From then on I spent countless hours at Whitchurch, usually watching the activity from a vantage-point in the Whitchurch–Bishopsworth lane. This was the closest I could get to the parked aircraft, and it was there, painted in large letters on two buildings, that I saw the names 'Airwork' and 'Norman Edgar'. They were probably among the first words that I learned to read and write. Between aircraft movements I enjoyed watching the skylarks and lapwings that frequented the surrounding fields of Pigeonhouse, Hengrove, and Inns Court Farms. And from those same fields, from about the age of ten, I flew rubber-powered model aircraft that I spent much time making. Flying was in my young blood, and for many years Whitchurch was the centre of my unswerving interest. More than that, it was the magical place where a boyhood dream – to one day become the captain of an airliner – eventually became reality. In my eyes, then as now, Whitchurch Airport was a fascinating place, and this book is the result.

Ken Wakefield

CHAPTER ONE

A Far Sighted Move

1927–1929

An *Airport Road* many miles from the nearest airport – and a nearby public house called *Happy Landings* – must surely puzzle strangers to the south Bristol districts of Knowle and Hengrove. To local elders, however, they are reminders that these suburbs were once dominated by Britain's most important international airport. It was a distinction earned during the darkest days of World War Two, when its rôle as the country's main air gateway to the free world was a closely guarded secret. At the time, news reports covering the arrival of Very Important Persons mentioned only an aerodrome "somewhere in the West Country", but many must have guessed that this was, in fact, Bristol (Whitchurch) Airport.

Eventually hemmed in by housing estates on three sides, and with Dundry Hill to the south, Whitchurch Airport, as it was more generally known, was incapable of expansion to meet post-war needs and in 1957 it closed in favour of a new airport at Lulsgate Bottom. Houses and an industrial estate featured in development plans for the old airport, but recreational needs were also taken into consideration, with the result that much of the original grass landing area and some of the former tarmac runway were retained as part of a new Hengrove Park and Whitchurch Sports Centre. In 1994 plans were approved to transform the park into a £15 million leisure and business complex, but in the meantime outdoor activities continued, with para-sailing and model aircraft flying maintaining an appropriate if tenuous link with the past. But that past is not only centred on wartime events, for Whitchurch also played an important part in the earlier 'Golden Age' of British civil aviation.

Looking at the vast housing estates which now spread southwards to the lower slopes of Dundry Hill, it is difficult to imagine that when it first opened Whitchurch Airport was deep in the countryside. This was in 1930 and followed an approach to Bristol City Council by the Bristol and Wessex Aeroplane Club. Formed in 1927 with two aircraft, the Club occupied premises at Filton, the factory airfield of the Bristol Aeroplane Company (BAC), but by 1929 the Club was seeking a new home. It was then operating four aircraft* and Club flying on this scale

**In June 1929 the Club's fleet consisted of a Parnall Pixie, G-EBKK, and three de Havilland DH 60X Moths, G-EBXF, G-EBYH and G-EBTV. By the end of the year it was also operating a Bristol Brownie, G-EBJL, and a DH 60M Moth, G-AASR.*

A Cirrus Moth of the Bristol and Wessex Aeroplane Club on snow covered Filton aerodrome during the winter of 1929–30. (P Dobbs)

was considered incompatible with the test and training flying then being carried out at Filton by the BAC and the resident RAF Reserve Flying School. Accordingly, with a view to finding a more suitable home – and with a municipal airport in mind – the Club made its approach to Bristol City Council. It was to be a far sighted move.

To examine and report on the matter an Airport Committee was formed under the chairmanship of Alderman A A Senington. Its other Members were the Lord Mayor (Councillor Walter Bryant), Aldermen A Dowling and H C Woodcock, and Councillors R Ashley Hall, H R Griffiths, R F Lyne, F Berriman, J E Jones, A L H Smith and J Owen. In May 1929, acting upon the recommendations of this Committee, the City Council decided to proceed with the project. A suitable site was soon found and subsequent negotiations resulted in Bristol Corporation purchasing 298 acres of land from Filwood and Tyning Farms at a cost of £52 per acre.

In November 1929 work commenced on clearing the landing area, advantage being taken of an unemployment relief scheme then in force, and construction of a Club House and other buildings followed. However, the Club's move from Filton, planned for December and then put back to January 1930, was further postponed until February because of bad weather. That same month the City Council, as administrators of the airport, appointed Captain Lea P Winters, the Secretary of the Bristol and Wessex Aeroplane Club, to the position of Airport Manager. Captain Winters was to continue with the Club and in this dual role he was responsible to a Management Committee whose

Members represented both the Corporation and the Club. The Chairman of this Committee was Alderman Richard Ashley Hall who, with Mr Arthur Taylor (Hon Financial Advisor), Cyril F Uwins and Leonard M Leaver, represented the Bristol and Wessex Aeroplane Club, Ltd. Members representing Bristol Corporation were Alderman Senington, Alderman A Dowling and Councillor A L H Smith.

1930

The first aircraft to land at the new airport was a de Havilland DH 60 Moth (G-EBXF), flown in from Filton on 4 February 1930 and followed in due course by the rest of the Club fleet and several privately owned aircraft. Another early arrival was a Gipsy Moth (G-AARA) owned by Merlyn Motors, Ltd., whose showrooms in Whiteladies Road, Bristol, incorporated a newly formed aircraft sales department managed by Mr Norman Edgar. The company had previously displayed a Moth in its Bristol premises, but aircraft sales were to be transferred to Whitchurch when an airport showroom was completed. Two other early Whitchurch residents were Gipsy Moths G-AAHF and G-AALV, owned

As it was in the beginning . . . the fields that later became Bristol (Whitchurch) Airport. (Wessex Airways)

The Club House under construction at Whitchurch, January 1930. (Bristol Times & Mirror)

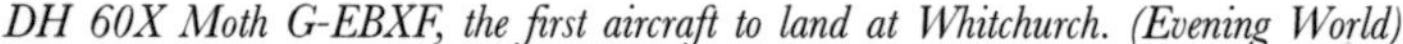

DH 60X Moth G-EBXF, the first aircraft to land at Whitchurch. (Evening World)

Another early arrival at Whitchurch was Cirrus Moth G-EBTV. (P Dobbs)

An interior view of the public hangar in February 1930, with Parnall Pixie III G-EBKK, four Moths and an Avro Avian. (Evening World)

respectively by the Hon Henry C H Bathurst and Mr A H Downes Shaw, the Club Chairman. Unfortunately, G-AAHF was shortly to be written off in a crash near Croydon, but its owner escaped unhurt.

The world famous Moth was the most commonly seen aircraft at Whitchurch in those early days and it was an aircraft of this type which carried out the first commercial flights from the airport. This was G-AAJS, a Gipsy Moth owned by Evening World-Northern Newspapers and chartered on several occasions by the Bristol Evening World before the airport was officially opened in May.

With the exception of nearby Dundry Hill (545-ft above airport level), with the distinctive landmark of Dundry church tower on its western brow, the approaches to Whitchurch were free of obstructions. The grass landing area was well drained and its dimensions were more than adequate for aircraft of the day. From the outset, provision was also made for an airport hotel, factory sites, a nine-hole golf course and future extension of the landing area. A passenger terminal was included in plans for the north side, adjacent to a proposed arterial ring road that was to encircle South Bristol, but for some time to come existing roads restricted building activity to the south-east corner of the airport, where the entrance was located. This was accessible only from the Whitchurch-Bishopsworth road, which was little more than a country lane intersected about mid-way between the two villages by another lane leading to Novers Hill and Parson Street, in the Bedminster district of Bristol. To replace these narrow approaches, which in winter-

Bristol 91B Brownie G-EBJL, with Merlyn's showroom still under construction. February 1930. (P Dobbs)

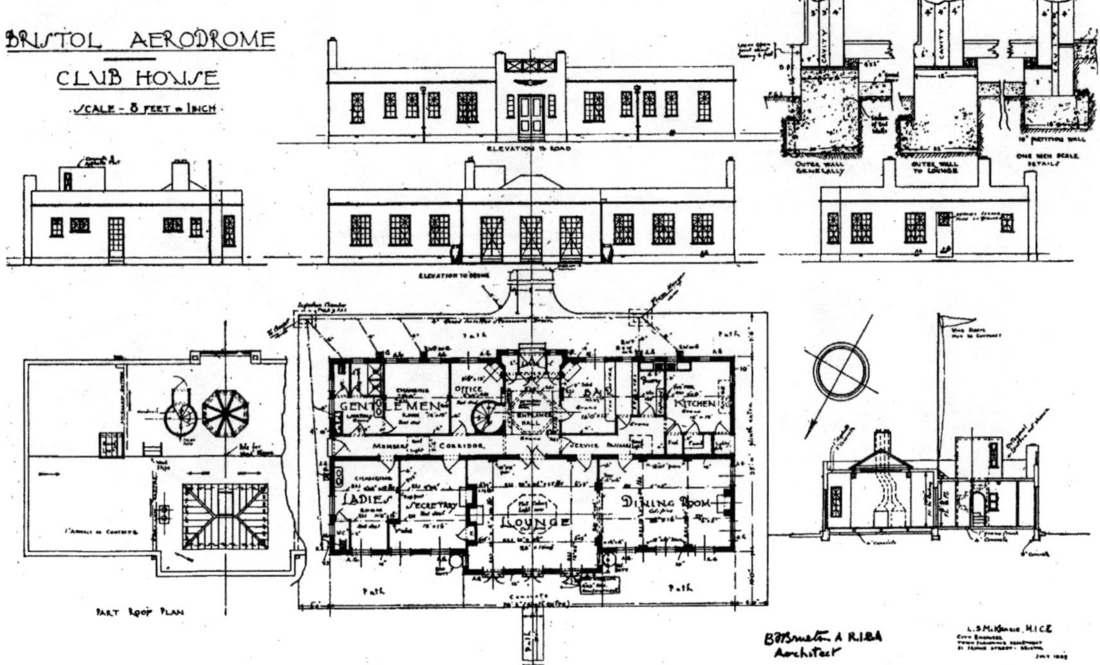

The architect's drawing of the Whitchurch Club House. (Author's Collection)

The Club House upon completion. Compare with the photo on page 4. (Bristol Times & Mirror)

The Club House lounge – art deco at its best. (Bristol Times & Mirror)

A 1930 Whitchurch line-up – Brownie G-EBJL and five DH Moths. (P Dobbs)

time were liable to flooding in places, a private road was to be built around the airport's eastern boundary to connect with the planned ring road (the Airport Road or A4174 of today). Construction of the latter began in April 1931, but it was not until 1933 that work commenced on the connecting private road. Meanwhile, before the airport was officially opened, a Club House, public hangar and showroom were completed in the attractive rural setting of the south-east corner, the steel framed buildings being constructed and erected by John Lysaught, Ltd., of Bristol.

Whitchurch, Britain's third municipally owned airport, was formally opened on 31 May 1930 by HRH Prince George, Duke of Kent. This was followed by an 'International Air Pageant', the occasion also marking the start of a British-French Week of celebrations. The Lord Mayor of Bristol was in attendance, together with the French Ambassador and some well known personalities including Will Hay, the film star comedian. Surprisingly, because of overcast skies with rain at times, some 30,000 spectators turned up, many of them pedestrians. There were comparatively few privately owned motor cars in those days, and people making the long walk to the 1/- (5p) public enclosure came by way of Novers Hill to Filwood Farm, or along footpaths leaving Bristol in Redcatch Road, Knowle, and in St John's Lane, near Victoria Park. Another approach was available from the bottom of Red Lion Hill, Knowle, along Hengrove Lane and through Tyning Farm.

The 1930 Moth fleet of the Bristol and Wessex Club – G-EBXF, G-EBTV, G-EBYH and G-AASR. (P Dobbs)

Two Moths and the Brownie in the public hangar. (P Dobbs)

DH 60M Gipsy Moth G-AASR of the Bristol and Wessex Aeroplane Club. (W K Kilsby)

Initially the buildings at Whitchurch consisted only of the Club House, hangar and showroom, as seen here. (Evening World)

For their pains the spectators were treated to a fine Pageant that included the Bristol Aerial Derby, an event won by Squadron Leader H M Probyn flying Westland Widgeon III G-EBRQ. Some of the other competitors were Cyril F Uwins, the BAC's Chief Test Pilot, flying the civil registered Bristol Bulldog G-ABAC, Mr A Gordon Store in Breda 15 G-AAVL, and Flight Lieutenant T B Bruce in DH 53 Humming Bird G-EBXN. Visiting aircraft included Avro Avian III G-EBVZ, shortly to win the 1930 King's Cup Air Race in the hands of Miss Winifred Spooner, several DH Moths and single examples of the Parnall Elf, Westland Wessex, Simmonds Spartan and Blackburn Bluebird.

Also present were two 'giant airliners', a Lioré-et-Olivier LeO 213 (F-AJNS, named *The Golden Ray*) of the French airline Air Union (the predecessor of Air France) and Handley Page W.8B G-EBBI *Prince Henry* owned by Imperial Airways but on hire to Captain C D Barnard's Aviation Tours, Ltd. Before and after the Pageant, and throughout the following day, the W.8B was used for 'joy-rides', as were the red Avro 504s of the Cornwall Aviation Company, which normally plied their trade that summer from a field at Locking Road, Weston-super-Mare. Although the Whitchurch joy-rides were quite expensive – 10s.6d (52½p) for a flight in the 12-passenger 'Imperial Airways Liner' and 6s. 0d (30p) for the three-passenger Avros – there was no shortage of customers, despite widespread unemployment and the low wages of many with jobs (£2–£3 per week for the so called average working man).

The first aircraft accident at Whitchurch occurred less than a month

A 1930 photo of the recently completed aircraft showroom of Merlyn Motors. (Evening Times & Echo)

A May 1930 view of the Whitchurch–Bishopsworth lane, looking towards the airport from the direction of Whitchurch village. Until April 1933 this was the main approach road to the airport. (R Winstone)

Another view of the Whitchurch–Bishopworth lane, looking towards the airport with Court Farm to the left. (A J Pitchers)

A reverse view of the previous photo, looking towards Whitchurch village from the direction of the airport. Beyond the bend the road slopes downhill and swings left to become the Ridgeway Lane of today. (A J Pitchers)

The first commercial flights from Whitchurch were carried out by Moth G-AAJS on charter to the Bristol Evening World. (Evening World)

The Duke of Kent at Whitchurch for the official opening ceremony on 31 May 1930, with the Lord Mayor of Bristol (right) and Mr A Downes-Shaw, Chairman of the Bristol and Wessex Aeroplane Club. (Flight)

after its official opening. This was on 22 June, when Moth G-EBZZ crashed while practising for the forthcoming King's Cup Air Race, injuring its pilot, Capt R S Rattray. The actual race took place on 5 July, with Whitchurch a control point at which all 88 competing aircraft were required to land, and this again drew a big crowd. Later that month another large contingent of aircraft arrived, but this time they were mainly foreign machines from Saint-Inglevert, participating in an International Air Touring Competition that started and finished at Berlin.

Another event during the airport's first year of operation was the Bristol and Wessex Aeroplane Club's Garden Party, held on 6 September. Will Hay, an enthusiastic amateur pilot and the owner of Puss Moth G-AALR, was again in attendance and came third in a flour-bag 'bombing' competition. Taking advantage of the meeting, Capt Hubert Broad, the de Havilland Company test pilot, demonstrated a Puss Moth to a group of prospective customers, among them Norman Edgar of Merlyn Motors, the local DH distributor. Also on view, and of special interest to many, was the Cierva C.19 Mk IV autogiro G-AAYP. The Garden Party, in effect a private air display and social gathering in pleasant surroundings, was considered a great success and was to become an annual event.

Air travel at this time was extremely limited, both by cost and by the few services available. Transport aircraft were lacking in mechanical reliability, and without radio navigation aids and reliable 'blind flying'

An admission ticket for the opening day Air Pageant. (M J Tozer Collection)

№ 58

BRISTOL AIR PORT.

International Air Pageant

and R.A.F. Display

MAY 31st, 1930.

2/6 ENCLOSURE (including Tax.)

Competitors for the Bristol Aerial Derby on opening day included (left to right) Humming Bird G-EBXN, Avian III G-EBVZ, two unidentified Moths (Cirrus and Gipsy powered), Breda 15 G-AAVL, Widgeon G-AAJF and Bulldog II G-ABAC. (Flight)

One of the largest aircraft present on Opening Day was this 18-passenger LeO 213 of the French airline Air Union. (I Peters via Mac Hawkins)

An early visitor to Whitchurch was DH 53 Humming Bird G-EBXN of the Royal Aircraft Establishment Aero Club, Farnborough. (M J Tozer Collection)

instruments they were severely restricted by adverse weather. Standards of safety, punctuality and regularity left much to be desired, but despite these problems Croydon-based Imperial Airways was gradually opening up mail and passenger services to Europe and many parts of the then mighty British Empire. Passengers, however, were generally both brave and wealthy. On the domestic scene several small companies were attempting to operate scheduled services, mainly across estuaries and to islands off mainland Britain, but it was air 'taxis', including aircraft chartered by newspapers, that brought the first commercial flights to Whitchurch.

Largely thanks to the efforts of Sir Alan Cobham – at first with a series of flights around Britain to promote a municipal airports scheme and then with his National Aviation Day Air Displays – the British public was fast becoming air minded. Interest was also stimulated by the daring exploits of Amy Johnson and other long-distance record breakers, and by the visits of small itinerant air circuses and organisations like Surrey Flying Services and the Cornwall Aviation Company, which offered 5s (25p) joy-rides. Unfortunately, in the economic depression of the time, few could afford to learn to fly; with charges in the order of £2 an hour it was a rich man's sport. Nevertheless, the Bristol Club and the airport it managed remained viable and continued to operate successfully.

In September 1930 Airwork, Ltd., a major aircraft maintenance and sales company based at Heston, London's second airport, opened a Service Depot at Whitchurch. Initially it occupied part of the public

DH test pilot Capt Hubert Broad and Norman Edgar, the local DH distributor (second from right) discuss the new Puss Moth with potential buyers. 6 September 1930. (Wessex Airways)

Hubert Broad displays the Puss Moth during the Garden Party on 6 September 1930. (Wessex Airways)

hangar, but the company had plans to erect its own hangar in the very near future. In the meantime work continued on other buildings and November saw the completion of two Wakefield 'cottages' at the airport entrance. Named after their architect, these were semi-detached houses built by Bristol Corporation for the Caretaker (Foreman Groundsman) and Club Steward, but their completion brought many enquiries from enthusiastic Club members eager to buy or rent houses near the airport.

By the end of the year, by which time Whitchurch had become a Customs Airport, seven private aircraft were in residence. An eighth, abandoned since the opening air pageant in May, was Mr Dudley Watt's DW 1, a modified World War I SE 5a fighter (registered G-EBOG) which remained at Whitchurch until 1932 when it was finally declared derelict and burnt.

CHAPTER TWO

The Early Thirties

1931

Shortly before Christmas 1930 two Moths belonging to the Bristol and Wessex Club were slightly damaged in a taxying collision, but a potentially more serious incident occurred on 14 February 1931 when one of these aircraft, Cirrus Moth G-EBYH, suffered an engine failure. In the forced landing which ensued, the Moth was again slightly damaged, but neither the pupil pilot nor Captain R W M 'Jimmie' Hall, who had recently become Chief Flying Instructor (CFI) in place of Mr E B W Bartlett, were hurt. One wing of the Moth struck overhead wires when it came down in a small field between the airport and Whitchurch village, but the damage was quickly repaired.

Ever intent on providing improved social facilities for its members, the Club commenced work on a squash court in March 1931 and this was later followed by a tennis court. On the flying side, a new Spartan Arrow (G-ABKL) arrived on 4 April as a replacement for Cirrus Moth G-EBYH, which then went to Norman Edgar for disposal. However, the Arrow failed to achieve the popularity of the Moths and it was sold the following year.

Airwork staff moved into their new hangar on 7 April, followed on 15 May by a formal key handing over ceremony performed by Alderman Senington of the Airport Committee and attended by Nigel Norman and Roderick Denman of Airwork. Previously, during another

The Airwork hangar under construction, April 1931. (Wessex Airways)

The formal opening of Airwork's hangar on 15 May 1931 with (left to right) Capt Lea P Winters (Airport Manager), Nigel Norman and Roderick Denman of Airwork and Alderman A A Senington, Chairman of the Airport Committee. The aircraft is Desoutter Mk I G-AAVO of Bristol Air Taxis. (Evening World)

Cirrus Moth G-EBTV receiving attention following damage to its tailskid while landing at Whitchurch. (P Dobbs)

ceremony on 18 April, the breaking of a bottle of cider on a propeller hub marked the start of operations by Bristol Air Taxis (BAT). Operating a Desoutter Mk II aircraft (G-AAVO), with Stephen B Cliff as pilot-manager, BAT was a subsidiary of Phillips and Powis Aircraft (Reading), Ltd., of Woodley, Berkshire.

A unique occasion at Whitchurch on 25 April was an official reception given to No 501 (City of Bristol) (Bomber) Squadron, Auxiliary Air Force, by the Lord Mayor and Aldermen of Bristol. It was the first time that any city in the British Empire had given a civic reception *at its own municipal airport* to a squadron with which it was directly connected. Upon their arrival from Filton, the Westland Wapitis of the squadron carried out an impressive low level formation fly-past.

Other events at Whitchurch in 1931 included a Flying Meeting on 20 June that incorporated a London–Bristol Air Race and displays and joy-rides by Capt C D Barnard's Aerial Circus. The Circus included a Cierva C.19 Mk II (G-AAYP) and a Fokker F.VIIA (G-EBTS) named *The Spider*: the latter was flown by Capt Barnard but owned by Air Tours, Ltd. In July this same aircraft, still flown by Capt Barnard but now operated by the British Air Navigation Company (BANCo), carried out an experimental passenger service between Bristol and Cardiff. This was at the invitation of the Airport Committee and between 11 and 18 July four flights were made each day, carrying a total of 199 passengers who paid 15s (75p) for a one-way ticket or 27s.6d (£1.37½p) return.

The King's Cup Air Race on 25 July was well attended, as was the Garden Party on 26 September. Local aircraft sales were also very sat-

The launch of Bristol Air Taxis, 18 April 1931. Desoutter G-AAVO is christened by Mrs Senington, wife of the Airport Committee Chairman. (Wessex Airways)

Spectators and a Cierva C.19 Mk II Autogiro at the Summer Flying Meeting, 20 June 1931. (Flight)

Civilian Coupé Mk II G-ABNT, owned by Stephen Cliff of Bristol Air Taxis, 1931. (W K Kilsby)

Fokker F.VIIA G-EBTS The Spider *of the British Air Navigation Company, used on the experimental Bristol–Cardiff service in 1931. (W K Kilsby)*

Puss Moth G-ABFV of Norman Edgar Ltd. (W K Kilsby)

OPPOSITE *A 1931 Bristol Air Taxis advertisement. (Author's Collection)*

isfactory and in September Norman Edgar formed his own company to take over the DH Agency and showroom formerly leased to Merlyn Motors. Consequently, when the Bristol and Wessex Club decided to sell the Brownie at the end of the year, its disposal was handled by Norman Edgar, Ltd. This left members with two DH 60X Cirrus Moths, a DH 60M Gypsy Moth and a Spartan Arrow, but moves were afoot to standardise on the very popular Gipsy Moth.

1932

Early in 1932 the number of private aircraft based at Whitchurch increased with the arrival of a Gipsy II Moth and a Cirrus Moth, both machines being supplied by Norman Edgar. Lord Apsley, the Club's President, also took delivery of a Klemm L25-1 (G-AAHL), but it was written-off at Whitchurch on 27 February when it collided with a windsock. Undeterred, Lord Apsley continued to fly, aided and abetted by Lady Apsley who shared his enthusiasm, and later in the year he purchased Parnall Elf I G-AAFH, bringing the number of privately owned aircraft in residence to 15.

In March, with Club finances in good order, it was decided to replace the two long serving Cirrus Moths with new DH 60G Gipsy Moths (G-ABTP and G-ABWM). The year was further marked by four events of

DH 60G Gipsy Moth G-ABTP of the Bristol and Wessex Aeoplane Club, 1932. (W K Kilsby)

Whitchurch Airport, 1932. The former Merlyn's showroom now carries the name Norman Edgar. (W K Kilsby)

Handley Page W.10 G-EBMR, at Whitchurch with Sir Alan Cobham's National Aviation Day Air Display, 4 June 1932. (Evening World)

BRISTOL-CARDIFF DAILY

Cardiff in 20 minutes in fast enclosed cabin machines. No extra clothing necessary. Bus leaves Maple Leaf Booking Office, Tramways Centre, BRISTOL daily 10.30 a.m., 2.30 p.m.

12/6 SINGLE **22/6** RETURN

NOW AIR TAXIS ARE CHEAPER

For 8d. per mile (4d. Per Passenger mile) you can now hire a luxurious enclosed cabin machine to take you quickly to any part of the country. Nothing is more comfortable than air-travel, whilst journeys which normally take 2 days, can often be done in a day. Mileage is taken "as the crow flies."

AIRCRAFT

A large selection of second - hand machines always in stock. Authorized De Havilland Agents.

NORMAN EDGAR

BRISTOL AIR SERVICES

BRISTOL AIRPORT

Telephone 41133

A 1932 Norman Edgar advertisement. (Author's Collection)

The smallest aircraft in Sir Alan Cobham's display was Comper Swift G-ABPY. (Evening World)

G-AAAF, one of the joy-riding Avro 504Ks of the Cornwall Aviation Co, at Whitchurch as part of Cobham's 'circus'. (W E Chapman)

interest to Club members, the first being a Summer Flying Meeting on 4 June which featured Sir Alan Cobham's National Aviation Day display. Led by Handley Page W.10 G-EBMR, on lease from Imperial Airways, the NAD 'circus' included a new three-engined Airspeed Ferry (G-ABSI) Comper Swift G-ABPY and the joy-riding Avro 504s G-EBIZ and G-AAAF of the Cornwall Aviation Company.

The second big event of 1932 was the now usual involvement with the King's Cup Air Race, which took place in July, and this was followed by the visit of a group of nearly 60 foreign touring aircraft in September.

The fourth event of the year – perhaps better described as a non-event which turned out well in the end – occurred on 3 July, after the London agents for the German airship LZ127 *Graf Zeppelin* had failed to obtain permission for it to land at Whitchurch. The airship, which was on a tour of Britain, required a ground handling party of 250 men and Bristol Corporation felt it was unable to meet the costs involved. Instead, the airship carried out a low altitude cruise over Bristol and its environs, making a great impression in the process. Carrying 28 passengers and a crew of 40, the 772-ft long *Graf Zeppelin* had made 28 trans-Atlantic trips in the previous three years, cruising at 90 mph and taking 2-3 days to complete each crossing. The later *Hindenburg*, which was seen in the Bristol area in 1936, was bigger and even more spectacular, but its loss in America in 1937 was to sound the death knell of big passenger-carrying airships.

During the summer of 1932 Norman Edgar decided to expand his business to include an air taxi operation, the intention being to use the most suitable aircraft of those in his showroom at the time. He began

The ROP (Russian Oil Products) petrol pumps and Norman Edgar's showroom in June 1932, with Beardmore Wee Bee G-EBJJ, Parnall Elf I G-AAFH and Elf IIs G-AAIN and G-AAIO. (Flight)

on 13 September with a charter flight to Heston for chocolate makers J S Fry & Sons, Ltd., of Keynsham, near Bristol, using Puss Moth G-ABWZ flown by Mr W N L Cope. Two days later the company announced a new air taxi service, charging fourpence (1.6p) per passenger mile (8d per aircraft mile) and using two three-seat Puss Moths (G-ABWZ and G-ABEC). This was followed shortly afterwards by the introduction of a Bristol-Cardiff 'air ferry' for which purpose DH 83 Fox Moth G-ABY0 was purchased. Although the Bristol-Cardiff experimental flights by BANCo in 1931 had been of short duration only, they were sufficient to convince Norman Edgar that, given the right aircraft, the route had much potential. Accordingly, on 26 September he began a twice daily service with his new Fox Moth.

The small, rather cramped cabin of the Fox Moth could accommodate four passengers but restricting accommodation to three provided more comfort. Powered by a single 120 hp Gipsy II engine it was an extremely economical aircraft to operate, allowing Norman Edgar, who had been joined in February by Mr Nasmyth Shaw as co-director, to set the fares at 12s.6d (62½p) single and 22s.6d £1.12½p) return. This was less than the First Class railway fare and as a result the well supported service continued throughout the winter, with a temporary extension beyond Bristol to Bath (Lansdowne) in December. In addition, two Puss Moths (G-ABWZ and G-ABFV) were kept busy on taxi and charter work with a third (G-ABBS, believed to be a showroom air-

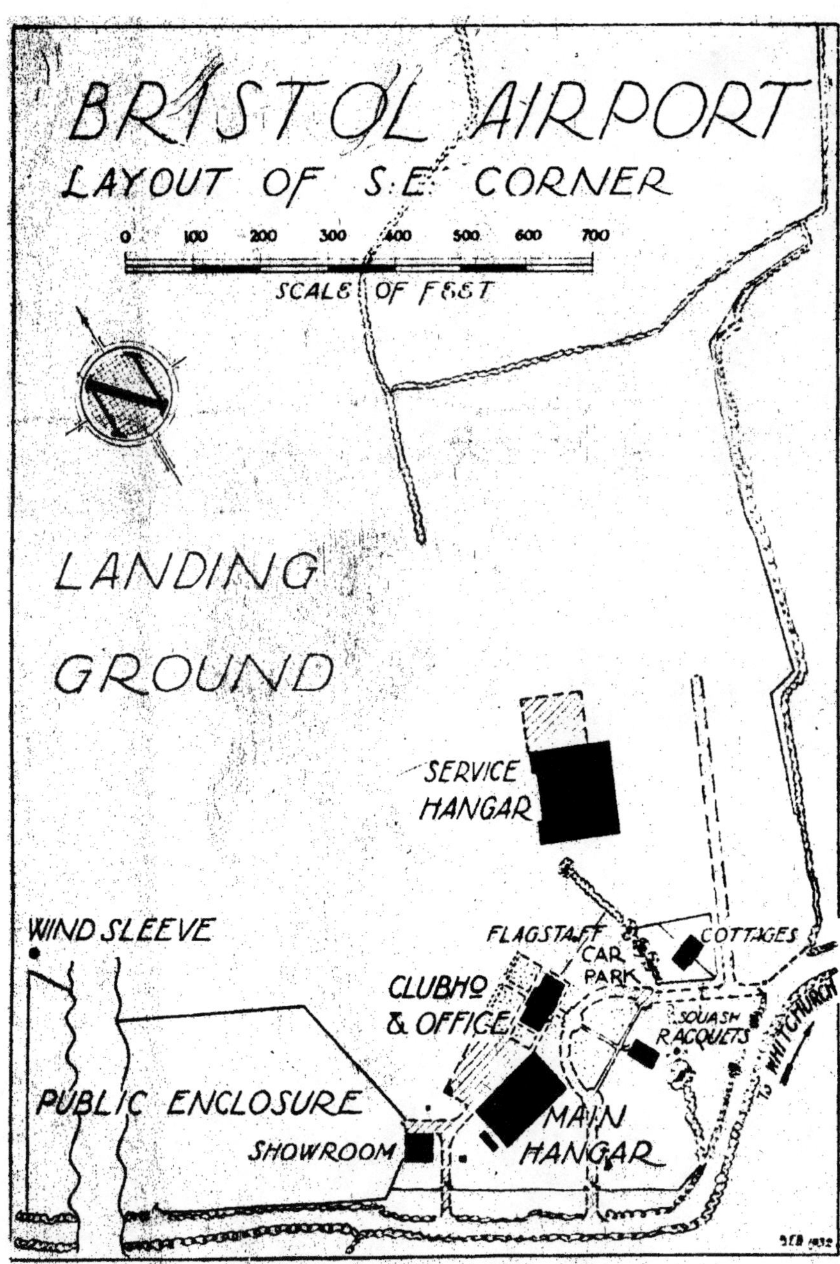

A sketch plan of the airport layout for the 1932 Air Pageant. (Wessex Airways)

craft awaiting a buyer) also temporarily available. The charter flying included a contract with J S Fry and Sons for a series of flights to Heston and elsewhere from a landing ground beside their Keynsham factory and to promote this operation Puss Moth G-ABWZ carried the Fry's logo. Several freelance pilots were employed by Norman Edgar, but most of the flying at this time was carried out by 'Spragg' Cope, an ex-RAF Flight Lieutenant who until September had been temporarily

The German airship Graf Zeppelin *over Bistol's city centre docks on Sunday, 3rd July 1932. (Port of Bristol Authority)*

Norman Edgar (right) with his newly acquired Fox Moth G-ABYO and Chief Pilot, Capt C R Cubitt. September 1932. (W K Kilsby)

employed by the Bristol and Wessex Aeroplane Club as assistant instructor.

It was a small beginning, but over the next six years Norman Edgar, an enthusiastic private pilot himself, was to expand his company's operations significantly. And in so doing he introduced thousands of people living in the West Country and South Wales to the advantages of air travel.

Less successful were the results achieved by Bristol Air Taxis, but this was not for lack of effort on the part of Stephen Cliff, the company's manager-pilot. BAT's two-passenger Desoutter was kept fairly busy with joy-rides and taxi work, including long distance charters to Naples in September 1932 and to Dusseldorf the following month, but the

The inaugural Bristol–Cardiff service, 26 September 1932. Norman Edgar assists the first two passengers, Mrs Fraser and daughter, to board Fox Moth G-ABYO. The pilot is F/O W N L Cope. (Evening World)

The Imperial Airways HP 42W G-AAXC Heracles, *flown by Capt O P Jones, landing at Whitchurch, 1 October 1932. (W K Kilsby)*

Despite drizzle and low cloud early in the day, the Club Garden Party on 1 October 1932 was an enjoyable occasion. Here the HP 42 towers above a variety of smaller aircraft. (W K Kilsby)

A typical 1937 scene at Whitchurch. (W K Kilsby)

demand for such work was insufficient to support two operators. Stephen Cliff had established an excellent reputation, but competition with Norman Edgar's expanding fleet eventually proved too much and Bristol Air Taxis ceased operations the following year.

As usual the Club's annual Garden Party, held on 1 October, was an enjoyable if rather damp affair, with low cloud and drizzle early in the day giving way to better conditions later on. In addition to Club machines numerous other aircraft were in attendance, but the highlight of the day was a visit by Handley Page HP 42W G-AAXC *Heracles* of Imperial Airways, flown from Croydon by the Bristol and Wessex Aeroplane Club's best known member, the already legendary Capt O P Jones.

1933

For much of early 1933 bad weather, including severe frost, hail and high winds, adversely affected flying, but over the Easter holiday the Bristol–Cardiff service was heavily booked and on two occasions extra flights were laid on. Arrangements were also in hand for flights to connect with a new Cardiff–Torquay–Teignnouth service to be operated by Imperial Airways on behalf of the Great Western Railway. The inaugural flight took place on 3 April, using the appropriately registered Westland Wessex G-AAGW. The six-passenger tri-motor aircraft, resplendent in the chocolate and cream colours of the GWR, was flown by Capt Gordon P Olley, one of Imperial Airways most experienced pilots. He was later to become very well known as the founder of Olley Air Service, Ltd. of Croydon.

April saw the completion of work started the previous November on the private road along the east boundary of the Whitchurch landing area. Linking up with the new arterial Airport Road, this greatly improved access to the airport from the A37 Wells Road at the bottom

The entrance to Whitchurch Airport in 1933, with hoardings advertising the Evening World *newspaper, the Grand Hotel, Grand Spa Hotel and Harvey's Bristol Milk Sherry. (L P Winters)*

DH 84 Dragon I G-ACJT of Norman Edgar (Western Airways) Ltd. (W K Kilsby)

Sir Alan Cobham's National Aviation Day Air Display used a variety of landing grounds in the West Country including the sands at Weston-super-Mare, where the joy-riding Handley Page Clive is here seen boarding passengers. (P Dobbs)

of Red Lion Hill. Little other construction work took place during the year although a concrete apron was laid adjacent to the Airwork hanger.

The 1933 Air Pageant, which again featured Sir Alan Cobham's NAD Air Display, took place on 17 June and was the highlight of Bristol–Brighton Week, a civic occasion linking the two towns. A week of excellent weather greatly facilitated a daily return service between Whitchurch and Brighton (Shoreham) by Norman Edgar, who obtained the use of the prototype Westland Wessex (G-EBXK) for the purpose, but on the day of the Pageant high winds and showers made things difficult for participating aircraft. Presumably because of the weather, only 5,000 spectators turned up, although it was estimated that another 10,000 watched the display from outside the airport without paying for admission.

The Pageant was opened by the Rt Hon Sir Phillip Sassoon, the Under Secretary of State for Air, who arrived from Northolt in a Hawker Hart of No 24 (Communications) Squadron, escorted by two more Harts. During the afternoon eight contestants competed for the Society of British Aircraft Constructors' Trophy in a race from Shoreham to Whitchurch, the winner being R F Hall in a Moth of the Lancashire Aero Club. Participants in the customary mass flypast were a Puss Moth, Blackburn Bluebird, Spartan Arrow, Fox Moth, Humming Bird, Wessex, Junkers F13 (G-ABDC of Brooklands Airways),

A 1933 Norman Edgar advertisement. (Wessex Airways)

The Circus comes to town, 17 June 1933. The opening fly-past at Whitchurch, with Sir Alan Cobham's HP Clive leading a Dragon, an Airspeed Ferry, two Avro 504s, three Avro Cadets, a Tiger Moth and a Puss Moth. (I Peters via Mac Hawkins)

Ford 4AT-E Trimotor G-ACAK at Whitchurch, 17 June 1933. (I Peters via Mac Hawkins)

Cobham's joy-riding Airspeed Ferry G-ABSI, seen here at Whitchurch with Comper Swift G-ABPY. (I Peters via Mac Hawkins)

Ford 4AT-E Trimotor (G-ACAK owned by the Ford Motor Company) and a Dragon. Display items included an 'attack' by three Bulldogs of No 3 (Fighter) Squadron on a Boulton Paul Sidestrand day bomber of No 101 Squadron, 'crazy' flying by a Club Moth, two parachute descents, and aerobatic displays by Nigel Tangye in a Comper Swift and Cyril Uwins in a Bristol Bulldog fighter. Other items were 'air drill' by Westland Wallaces of No 501 Squadron, and an autogiro demonstration by R A C 'Reggie' Brie of the Cierva company. Joy-rides were available throughout the day in Norman Edgar's Fox and Puss Moths, the Junkers F.13 of Brooklands Airways, and most of the NAD Display aircraft. The latter included a 10-passenger Airspeed Ferry and a 22-passenger Handley Page Clive, Cobham's latest 'Giant Airliner'. All went well, but while the Pageant was in progress a Percival Gull flown by designer Edgar Percival arrived and proceeded to carry out an impressive display. The impromptu performance was well received by the crowd, but less so by the organisers of what, until then, had been a well planned and carefully timed sequence of events. Nevertheless, it was a generally pleasing day.

Less pleasing for the Club was an incident that occurred on 21 June. This was the arrival in High Street, Yatton, of its Gipsy Moth G-ABWM, apparently the result of a forced landing. Luckily the aircraft was only slightly damaged and its pilot, a Mr Jall Sorabjee, was unhurt – until, that is, the arrival of a Club instructor, according to the Club's newsletter!

Well known visitors on 11 July were Mr and Mrs James Mollison who flew a Puss Moth from Whitchurch to visit Mr C P T Hulm at Heston, where the latter was preparing for a transatlantic flight. Mrs Mollison

The prototype Westland Wessex EBXK at Whitchurch during the Bristol–Brighton Week civic link-up in June 1933. (I Peters via Mac Hawkins)

Sir Alan Cobham's Handley Page Clive G-ABYX at Whitchurch, 17 June 1933. (I Peters via Mac Hawkins)

Junkers F.13ge G-ABDC of Brooklands Airways at Whitchurch, 17 June 1933. (I Peters via Mac Hawkins)

Refuelling Blackburn F.2A Lincock G-AALH during the NAD Air Display at Whitchurch, 17 June 1933. National Benzole Mixture is being dispensed from a Leyland Cub lorry. (I Peters via Mac Hawkins)

Westland Wallaces of No. 501 (City of Bristol) (Bomber) Squadron make a low fly-past over Whitchurch, 17 June 1933. (Evening World)

Moth G-ABWM after an unscheduled arrival in the High Street, Yatton, on 21 June 1933. (Evening World)

The Hon H C Bathurst (right), winner of the Garden Party landing competition, receives his prize from Mr A H Downes-Shaw, Chairman of the Bristol and Wessex Club, with Capt C D Barnard and Mr R Ashley Hall in attendance. 16 September 1933. (Evening World)

was, of course, the former Miss Amy Johnson of record breaking fame, and she and her husband were themselves planning to cross the Atlantic from East to West. They eventually did so on 22 July, taking off from Pendine Sands, South Wales, in the specially modified Dragon G-ACCV *Seafarer,* which had earlier passed through Whitchurch.

The weather was superb for the Garden Party in September when, once again, the Wallaces of No 501 Squadron performed. That same month the business of Norman Edgar, Ltd., was taken over by a new company registered as Norman Edgar (Western Airways), Ltd. With a capital of £7,500 in £1 shares and an office in Denmark Street, Bristol, the directors were listed as Norman W G Edgar, Leslie J Arnott and David B Gray. Coincidentally with these changes the company's pilots began wearing uniform, with Captain C R Cubitt (late of No 43 Squadron, RAF) as Chief Pilot. Further, a new DH 84 Dragon, G-ACJT, was added to the existing fleet of two Puss Moths and a Fox Moth. Flown by the Chief Pilot, the Dragon operated its first Bristol-Cardiff service on 15 September.

Charter or air taxi services were also developing satisfactorily and by the end of the year, with the demise of Bristol Air Taxis, Norman Edgar (WA) Ltd., was doing most of the taxi work from the airport. Charters included a Dragon flight to Stoke-on-Trent with wireless sets and spare parts, and trips with the Fox Moth to Manchester with 224 lbs of chocolates, to Birmingham with 168 lbs of chocolates, and to Birmingham again with 336 lbs of cocoa. Aircraft sales were also satis-

Dragon I G-ACJT of Norman Edgar (Western Airways) Ltd with (left to right) Norman Edgar, Chief Pilot C R Cubitt, F/O G W Monk and Lt Col Gray, OBE, MC (director). September 1933. (W K Kilsby)

Still in its J S Fry & Sons logo, Puss Moth G-ABWZ takes to the road, hauled by a tractor of Joseph Fish and Sons, Ltd, the motor transport contractors of Victoria Street, Bristol. (M J Tozer Collection)

Norman Edgar's Puss Moth G-ABWZ while on charter to J S Fry & Sons Ltd, with the chocolate company's name on its engine cowling. (M J Tozer Collection)

An RAF visitor. A Bristol Bulldog of No. 3 (Fighter) Squadron, flanked by Norman Edgar's Fox and Puss Moths, with the Airwork hangar in the background. The Avro 504 beyond the Fox Moth belonged to the Cornwall Aviation Company. (M J Tozer Collection)

factory; earlier in the year the company delivered five aircraft in the space of only a few weeks, including new machines to Sir Philip Sassoon, Lord Borodale and Mr Loel Guinness. In addition Puss Moth G-ABEL was sold to Mr Howard Darren, and a Blackburn Bluebird and Gipsy I Moth went to customers in France. Then came the sale of two Percival Gulls, followed in October by a deal with Mr S H Binning, a new member of the Bristol and Wessex Club who bought a Gipsy II Moth to celebrate his first solo flight.

The future of aviation in the West Country was looking assured and by the end of 1933 the number of people employed at the airport had risen to 35, Airwork being the biggest employer with 15 people working in its Service Depot.

1934

On 20 January 1934 Norman Edgar launched what was probably the world's first airline shuttle service, with hourly departures between Bristol and Cardiff. The occasion was connected with a Wales-England International Rugby Match in Cardiff and the flights were laid on to meet public demand. Shortly after this the Dragon was chartered by a group of Welsh miners to fly them from Tylerstown to Edinburgh for a Scotland-Wales rugby match, but fog intervened and the miners settled instead for a soccer match at Portsmouth. Continuing the company's involvement with sport, several aircraft were also used to take Bristol Rovers Football Club to the Welsh capital for a game with Cardiff City.

An unsual aircraft at Whitchurch in 1934 was the Shackleton Murray SM.1 G-ACBP owned by Lord Apsley, President of the Bristol Club. (P Dobbs)

Cierva C.30A Autogiro G-ACXP was operated by the Bristol Club at Whitchurch from September to December 1934. (W K Kilsby)

New types of commercial aircraft at this time included the Short Scion and on 14 March 1934 an aircraft of this type was demonstrated to Norman Edgar. However, his company, now better known simply as Western Airways, was to remain faithful to de Havilland for its equipment. Indeed, only the Dragon could offer lower seat costs per mile than the Fox Moth, which itself was an airline accountant's dream come true.

On 13 May the Western Airways Dragon, flown by a Major Ropner, inaugurated a 'Sunshine Air Express' service from Bristol to Bournemouth, from where connections were available to other destinations including the Channel Islands. Unfortunately, shortly after this development the Company suffered its first accident, losing Fox Moth G-ABYO in a crash at Chepstow on 16 June. The pilot, Douglas Brecknell, rescued two passengers from the blazing aircraft, which was also carrying a cargo of wireless sets from Cardiff to Bristol.

Passenger services from Whitchurch were further expanded in 1934 with Railway Air Services arriving on the scene. A recently organised subsidiary of Imperial Airways, RAS was formed jointly with the main railway companies to operate internal air services. It was to develop an extensive route network, at first mainly with Dragons, to become the principal British domestic airline. The main base of the new company was Croydon, but its arrival at Whitchurch was in connection with a peak summer service between Birmingham and Cowes (Isle of Wight),

Moth Major G-ACPT was delivered to the Bristol and Wessex Club in June 1934. (W K Kilsby)

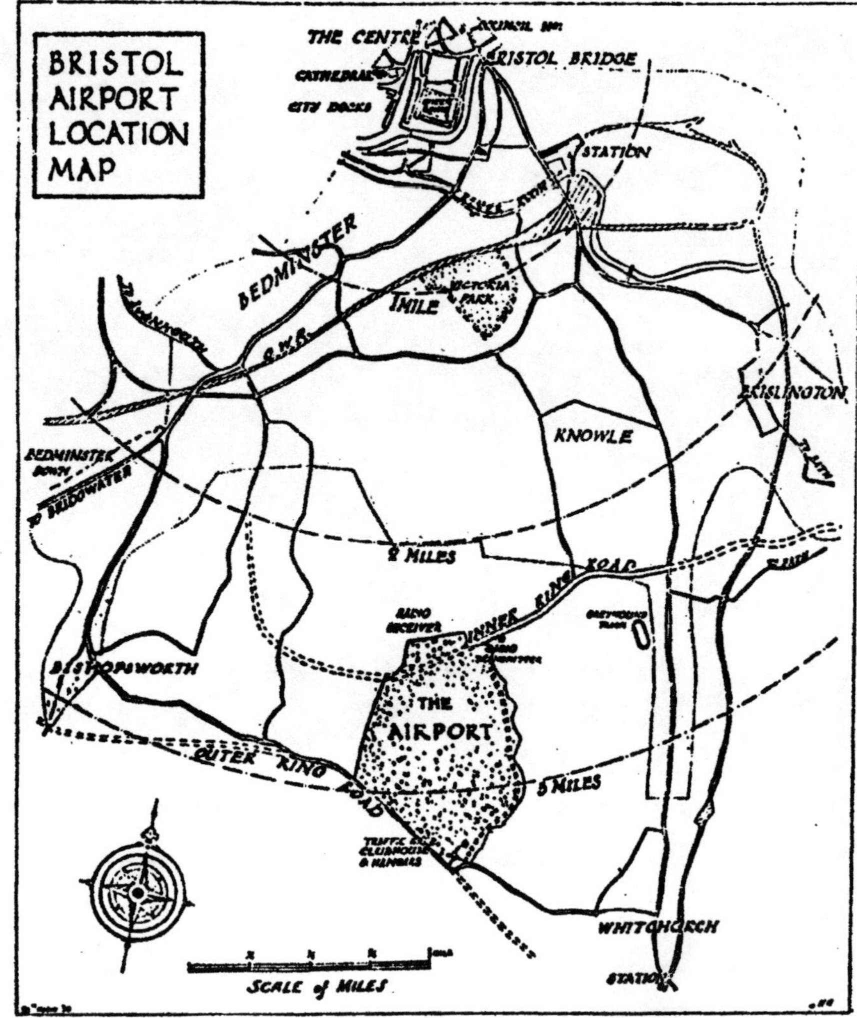

A sketch map published in 'Wessex Airways', the Club's newsletter, showing the location of the airport.
(Wessex Airways)

with intermediate stops at Bristol and Southampton. A Dragon II was used and from 20 August mail was carried on the route, the Bristol–Birmingham sectors being flown both ways that day by F/Lt G H Sender. On the same day Capt Cubitt completed the first airmail flight by Western Airways from Bristol to Cardiff.

The new RAS service was typical of those operated by domestic airlines at that time. With few exceptions they were short over-water crossings, were usually seasonal and, like a country bus service, stopped frequently along the way. Western Airways was less seasonal than most airlines, its Bristol–Cardiff service operating all year round but at a reduced frequency, or 'on demand' only, during the winter months. However, in the summer peak period two of the four daily flights continued beyond Bristol to Bournemouth (Christchurch). Introduced on a seasonal basis, this extension ceased at the end of September, but until then it offered a connection with the Brighton (Shoreham)–Portsmouth

The 'Airway Express' 14-seater bus, about to leave the Tramways Centre for the airport. (M J Tozer Collection)

The end of the route. The white-painted special airport bus at Whitchurch, with a Dragon of Western Airways. (M J Tozer Collection)

RAILWAY
AIR
SERVICES

De Havilland Dragon 8-Seater Twin-Engined Aeroplane as operating on the Plymouth—Liverpool and Cowes—Birmingham Services

PLYMOUTH, TEIGNMOUTH, CARDIFF BIRMINGHAM and LIVERPOOL.

COWES (I. of W.), SOUTHAMPTON BRISTOL, BIRMINGHAM.

LONDON (Croydon) and ISLE of WIGHT

Full information from any G.W.R. or S.R. Station or Office, Principal L M S Stations and Travel Agents.

A Railway Air Services poster advertising the Cowes (Isle of Wight) service inaugurated on 30 July 1934. (Welsh Industrial & Maritime Museum)

–Bournemouth service flown by Portsmouth, Southsea and Isle of Wight Aviation, Ltd., with further connections at Portsmouth to Jersey and the Isle of Wight. At Cardiff, the Western Airways service from Bristol connected with the RAS Plymouth–Teignmouth (Haldon)–Cardiff service that was extended to Birmingham (Castle Bromwich) from 22 May.

On 31 July the Bristol Tramways & Carriage Company, in association with Western Airways, commenced a special bus service between the Tramways Centre and the airport via Temple Meads Railway Station. A specially fitted 14-seater bus, painted white to distinguish it from ordinary service buses, ran every day to a regular time-table, connecting with departures and arrivals at the airport and routing via Temple Meads to provide a complete rail, road and air link. The association between the two companies was further enhanced by Bristol Tramways acting as agents for the airline and handling bookings for all destinations through its principal offices in Bristol and branches at Weston-super-Mare, Wells, Gloucester and Cheltenham.

Despite the loss of its Fox Moth, by August 1934 Western Airways had covered some 40,000 miles on the Bristol–Cardiff ferry. All its departures had been on schedule, and in two years its Chief Pilot had made 1,000 crossings of the Bristol Channel. In addition to Capt Cubitt, two more ex-RAF pilots – K Maconochie and N F Henkel – were now employed by the company.

Good progress was also being maintained on the private flying scene and with a record year behind it the Bristol and Wessex Club was able to look again at the possibility of acquiring new aircraft. Thus, in April

The Lord Mayor of Bristol (Ald T Wise) receives the first air mail to arrive at Whitchurch, flown in from Cardiff by Capt Cubitt in a Dragon of Western Airways. 20 August 1934. (Evening World)

a new DH 60G-III Moth Major was ordered, but until its delivery in June a DH 82 Tiger Moth was provided on loan by the de Havilland Aircraft Company. With the arrival of the Moth Major (G-ACPT) it was decided to sell DH 60M G-AASR, which had been in service since 1929, but it remained with the Club until October.

Earlier, in March, Lord Apsley was in the news when his Parnall Elf I G-AAFH was damaged beyond repair while making a forced landing near Rickmansworth, Herts. However, in November the indomitable Bristol and Wessex Club President bought Parnall Elf II G-AAIN as a replacement. Although normally kept at Yate, this now very well known aircraft – 62 years on it is still flying with the Shuttleworth Collection at Old Warden – was frequently seen at Whitchurch.

The airport was opened to the public on Empire Air Day, 24 May, when the four-engined DH 86 Express G-ACPL *Diana*, painted in the livery of Railway Air Services, was displayed by Capt O P Jones of Imperial Airways. Other events at Whitchurch in 1934 were a visit by Sir Alan Cobham's 'circus' on 16 June (when Miss Joan Meakins set the Women's World Record for the number of loops performed successively in a glider), the Bristol Garden Party on 28 July, and C W A Scott's British Hospitals Air Pageant (which featured 'The Sky Devils' Air Circus') on 18 August.

In July Mr A H Downes-Shaw resigned as Club Chairman and was succeeded by Richard Ashley Hall, an Airport Committee Member and the first member of the Club to obtain an 'A' (Private Pilot's) Licence. Another development was the acquisition by the Club of a new Cierva C.39A Autogiro registered G-ACXP. This was in September and was thanks to a generous benefactor who wished to remain anonymous, but for some unknown reason it was sold in December to a buyer in Australia.

Another aircraft which took up residence at Whitchurch in 1934 was one of the new breed of low-wing monoplanes. This was Miles Hawk Major G-ACWY owned by Lady Blanche Douglas, a sister of the Duke of Beaufort. Having gained her 'A' Licence in June, it was her intention to fly the new aircraft to India in November, accompanied by Flying Officer C V Ogden, the assistant instructor who had been employed by the Club for the summer season.

CHAPTER THREE

The Mid Thirties

1935

Commercial operations from Whitchurch expanded quite rapidly in 1935. From 2 April, when the first service was flown by Capt Coates, Crilly Airways operated Dragon G-ACCZ on the route Norwich–Leicester–Bristol and on 15 May this was extended to include Plymouth. That same day a Bristol–Croydon and/or Heston service was also introduced by Crilly, and from 18 May the stop at Leicester provided connections to Nottingham, Doncaster and Northampton. In addition to Dragon I G-ACCZ, the Crilly fleet operating through Whitchurch included Dragon I G-ACDN and Monospar ST.25 Jubilees G-ADPK, G-ADPL and G-ADPM.

Railway Air Services also expanded its operations with a seasonal Liverpool–Birmingham–Bristol–Southampton–Portsmouth–Shoreham service, using two new Dragon IIs (G-ADDI *City of Cardiff* and G-ADDJ *City of Plymouth*). During the summer the Dragons were joined and eventually replaced by two new DH 89 Dragon Rapides (G-ACPP *City of Bristol* and G-ACPR *City of Birmingham*).

Gipsy Moth G-ABWM, Moth Major G-ACPT and an unidentified Gipsy Moth at Whitchurch in 1935. (W K Kilsby)

Purchased in May 1935, Avro 643 Cadet G-ADFD remained in service with the Bristol Club until the outbreak of war. (W K Kilsby)

To handle the increasing numbers of passengers a new terminal building, or Main Traffic Hall as it was called, was opened at Whitchurch in July. This replaced a temporary building erected in May, in which month Western Airways became an international airline. This was on the 3rd, when a Dragon flew the first weekend 'on demand' service from Cardiff to Paris (Le Bourget) via Whitchurch and Le Touquet. To meet its increased commitments for the 1935 summer season, the company was now operating two Puss Moths and three Dragons, including Dragon II G-ACMP on lease from Jersey Airways. However, on 22 July this aircraft crashed 1½ miles from Cardiff while on a flight from Bristol with Capt M J Mansfield in command. Western Airways then obtained a Dragon II G-ACPX as a replacement and later in the year also operated Dragon I G-ACAO, owned by Lady Apsley. Previously resident at the family home at Badminton but frequently seen at Whitchurch, this aircraft remained in service with Western Airways and was eventually purchased by the company in 1938.

The year 1935 also brought changes to the local private flying scene. In February 'Jimmie' Hall, the Bristol and Wessex Club's Chief Flying Instructor, left to join Imperial Airways and was replaced by Mr E M H Slade, who had been on a temporary contract with the Club in 1933 as assistant instructor. The following month an Avro 643 Cadet was

The BAC Drone was one of the aircraft featured by Sir Alan Cobham and other flying circuses in the mid-1930s. (I Peters via Mac Hawkins)

demonstrated to the Club by Henly's, Ltd., and those members given the opportunity to fly it were greatly impressed. Subsequently a Cadet was ordered for delivery in April, but it was not until 24 May that G-ADFD arrived, fully equipped for night flying.

Empire Air Day on 25 May was followed on 15 June by the race for a trophy presented by the Society of British Aircraft Constructors, but rain and high winds tended to spoil both events. Indeed, bad weather was to plague air displays at Whitchurch for some time to come.

An interesting visitor to the airport in 1935 was Robert Kronfeld's ultra light BAC Drone, flown from Hanworth on 12 April. A Swallow and an Eagle were also demonstrated by the British Aircraft Manufacturing Company, and an Aeronca C-3 was displayed by Light Aircraft, Ltd., the UK distributor of the American aircraft. But it was the Swallow, derived from a German Klemm design, that made the most favourable impression. Although the Swallow was a new type, its Klemm forebears had been on the Whitchurch scene for some time with Lord Apsley's German-built L27a-VIII G-ABOP based there since May. An L25C-IA, G-ACUF made under licence in Britain by the British Klemm Company and owned by Mr F L Gates, was also a resident. Later on, BA Swallows were to form a major part of the Bristol Club's fleet which, at the end of 1935 comprised a Cadet, two Gipsy Moths and a Moth Major.

Nearly all the flying on internal routes in the early days was carried out visually, with pilots remaining clear of cloud and in sight of the ground. No radio was carried and navigation depended on map reading and familiarity with the route. As a result bad weather, and especially low cloud, mist or fog, were major hazards which frequently disrupted schedules and caused a number of serious accidents, often with aircraft becoming lost and flying into high ground. By the mid-Thirties, however, suitably equipped aircraft were able to fix their position by means of bearings obtained from a slowly increasing number of ground communications and direction finding (D/F) stations. One of these was at Whitchurch, where work began in September 1935 on a permanent Marconi-Adcock D/F station. Replacing a temporary mobile unit, the new transmitter was located on the north boundary of the airport, with the receiver building and four 70-ft masts just outside the north-east corner. Operating on a frequency of 348 kc/s (862m), the radio telephony (R/T) call-sign was 'Bristol', with 'GJB' the three-letter Morse call-sign for wireless telegraphy (W/T) communications. Obviously, however, the system was available only to aircraft equipped with two-way radio, which in those days was bulky and required a Radio Officer to operate it. In Dragons and Dragon Rapides this meant the loss of at

Holiday-makers on a 'Mystery Tour' organised by Burnells Motors of Weston-super-Mare found themselves on a sight-seeing trip to Whitchurch. Three coach loads are seen here with two pilots of Western Airways and four DH Dragons. (M J Tozer Collection)

The three Burnells Motors' coaches which brought 'Mystery Tour' trippers from Weston-super-Mare to Whitchurch in May 1935. (M J Tozer Collection)

G-ADDI City of Cardiff, *one of two new Dragon IIs used by RAS on its services through Whitchurch in 1935. (Welsh Industrial & Maritime Museum)*

These four RAS aircraft – Dragon Rapides G-ACPR City of Birmingham *and G-ACPP* City of Bristol, *with Dragon IIs G-ADDI* City of Cardiff *and G-ADDJ* City of Plymouth – *were regular visitors to Whitchurch during the summer of 1935. (Welsh Industrial & Maritime Museum)*

least one passenger seat, with the result that few operators were prepared to install radio for use on short domestic flights. However, on major routes such as Croydon–Belfast, it permitted flight in or above cloud and did much to improve both safety and regularity.

In addition to the new wireless station, night-flying lighting was also completed at Whitchurch in September. Installed by the General Electric Company it comprised Chance flood lights, obstruction lights and an illuminated wind 'Tee' direction indicator. Night flying was still something of a novelty and Club members attending a Sherry Party and informal dance in October were able to sample night joy-rides in a Dragon of Western Airways flown by Mr R Barrett. At the same time the Club's CFI was busy giving night dual instruction in the Cadet up to 10.30 pm.

As the year came to a close a new company, Western Air Transport, was registered, its directors being those of Norman Edgar (Western Airways), Ltd. The company had no aircraft and did not operate as an airline, but no doubt Norman Edgar, a shrewd businessman, had good reason to register it. The late Richard Ashley Hall, then Chairman of the Bristol and Wessex Club and a member of the Airport Committee, knew Norman Edgar well and described him to the author as "... a bit of a rascal at times, but clever and likeable". To illustrate his point Ashley Hall (then a director of John Hall and Sons, the Bristol manufacturer of aircraft paints and dopes and a man who did much for civil aviation in the West Country) went on to relate what happened when his good friend Nigel Norman, the Managing Director of Airwork,

A close-up of four RAS aircraft (two Dragon Rapides and two Dragons) frequently seen at Whitchurch. (Welsh Industrial & Maritime Museum)

A Western Airways Dragon at Whitchurch, photographed from another Dragon of the same company, that has just arrived from the Isle of Wight via Bournemouth, 14 July 1935. (R Winstone)

came to see Norman Edgar about a long overdue bill. Maintenance of the latter's aircraft was being carried out by Airwork's Bristol Service Depot and apparently quite a large sum of money was owing. Prior to his confrontation with Edgar, Nigel Norman spent the night at Richard Ashley Hall's home in Chew Magna, where he spoke of his determination to obtain settlement of the bill in full. The following morning he drove off to meet Norman Edgar at Whitchurch in the same determined mood, only to return later in the day with the bill still unpaid and the airline's credit extended still further!

1936

During the financial year ending 31 March 1936, the total number of aircraft movements at Whitchurch was 4,810, with 6,003 passengers and 2,520 lbs of freight passing through the airport. These were excellent results and in April, no doubt influenced by anticipated further growth, the Airport Committee decided to terminate the airport's management by the Bristol and Wessex Club and instead exercise direct control. However, a development in February was to have some effect on traffic growth. That month work started on a new airport at Weston-super-Mare, from where Western Airways commenced a service to Cardiff in May. This was followed in June by the transfer of the airline's administrative office and main base from Whitchurch to Weston Airport, which the airline was to manage for the local authority.

By no means was aviation new to Weston, for as far back as 1911 an early aviator named Hucks had carried out a series of 'exhibition flights' – including the first aerial crossing of the Bristol Channel to Cardiff and back – from The Aviation Grounds, a field situated close to the old Locking Road Tram Terminus. More recently, joy-riding Avro 504s had flown from fields at Locking Road and near Brean, and on several occasions Sir Alan Cobham's circus had used Weston sands, with aircraft as big as the Handley Page Clive using the southern end of the beach near the Sanatorium, but the far sighted local council was determined to provide the Somerset holiday resort with a good permanent airport. A site at Hutton Moor was selected, but for a small town like Weston an airport was an expensive undertaking. However, the Council had every confidence in Norman Edgar, who had been working on the project for some years. Other important contributors to the venture were Mr E Macfarlane, chairman of the Weston Airport Committee, Mr Henry Butt, the charter-mayor-elect, Mr J G Western, chairman of the district council, and Mr Henry Brown, the town surveyor. Preparation of the landing area was carried out under the direction of the latter although, as at Whitchurch, the specialist knowledge of John Lysaught, Ltd., of Bristol was employed for the erection of a hangar.

Although the main base of Western Airways was now Weston, the company continued to operate through Whitchurch, but during the

BA Swallow II G-AEAV, used by the Bristol Club from February 1936 to September 1939. (W K Kilsby)

Stephen Appleby (centre) and his Flying Flea G-ADMH at Whitchurch, 28 March 1936. (Evening World)

summer it was carrying out 14 return flights each day between Cardiff and Weston compared with only three between Cardiff and Bristol. There were also three flights each day between Bristol and Weston.

In 1936 Crilly Airways continued to operate the services it had started the previous year and from 15 May extended them beyond Bristol to Plymouth. Further, in July it took over the Bristol–Bournemouth route formerly operated by Western Airways, but Crilly was running into financial difficulties and in September was taken over by British Airways, Ltd. With this development all existing Crilly Airways services through Bristol were abandoned.

To some degree the failure of Crilly was offset by the success of Irish Sea Airways (Aer Lingus Teoranta) with a daily Dublin (Baldonnel)–Bristol service using the DH 84 Dragon EI-ABI *Iolar.* The first service was flown on 27 May by Capt O G 'Paddy' Armstrong, the Company's Chief Pilot, and from the outset the route showed much promise. It was no surprise, therefore, when the Dragon was replaced by the four-engined DH 86 EI-ABK *Eire* and the route extended to Croydon from 14 September.

Railway Air Services opened its 1936 season with routes identical to those flown the previous year, but in May introduced a Manchester–Liverpool–Birmingham–Bristol–Southampton–Isle of Wight (Ryde)–Shoreham service. This was operated by Dragon Rapides from 25 May to 12 September, with request stops at Meir (for Stoke-on-Trent) and Staverton (for Gloucester and Cheltenham). RAS also began a Bristol– Weston–Cardiff–Plymouth service, using Dragons, with request stops at Exeter and Torquay. The Cardiff–Bristol sector was flown in direct competition with Western Airways and from 21 August

The Club apron at Whitchurch on a fine summer day in 1936. (Evening World)

RAS increased the frequency of its Cardiff–Weston service with hourly departures.

By early 1936 the Pou-du-Ciel or Flying Flea, the brain-child of Monsieur Henri Mignet, had taken the country by storm. A Flying Flea gathering and display at Whitchurch on 28 March added to the fervour, but the tiny build-it-yourself aeroplane that, according to the popular press, 'could be made from old orange boxes', was running into trouble. True, on this occasion Stephen Appleby put on a good display in his example, but few Flying Fleas built by enthusiasts did, in fact, fly. And those that did often crashed, sometimes taking their pilots to their deaths. Flying Fleas were eventually banned by the Air Ministry, but before this came about Whitchurch witnessed the spectacle of its first locally made specimen trying to get airborne.* This was on 7 May when, after several short hops, the Pou (G-AEHM) made by Mr H J Dolman turned over on its back. The intrepid Harry Dolman, a well known local businessman, escaped unhurt and his aircraft survives to this day; only slightly damaged, the Flea was presented to the Science Museum and now forms part of its unique aeronautical collection at Wroughton, Wilts.

In the meantime, in January 1936, the two Bristol Club Gipsy Moths

* *Following design changes the ban on flying was lifted and in recent years successful variations of the basic type have again become popular, with home construction carried out under an approved inspection scheme.*

The transatlantic Vultee V-IA NR13770 Lady Peace *at Whitchurch, 4 September 1936. (Evening World)*

Monospar ST.25 Jubilee G-AEDY and Taylor J2 Cub G-AEIK at the Garden Party, 5 September 1936. (Evening World)

were sold and replaced by two Pobjoy-powered BA Swallow IIs (G-AEAU and G-AEAV). The new aircraft were collected from the Hanworth factory on 31 January by the CFI and Mr A H Phillips, Chairman of the Flying Committee. Both were very experienced ex-Service pilots and both agreed it was a day which produced the worst weather either had known, with violent storms and a 60 mph headwind. But they were full of praise for their new aircraft, which went into service at very low hourly flying rates – £1.10s (£1.50p) solo, but only £1.7s (£1.35p) before 2 pm on any day except Sunday and Bank Holidays. The Moth Major was also sold in May, but the Cadet – now fitted with a hood for 'blind flying' training – was retained. Enclosed cabin aircraft were becoming increasingly popular with private owners, however, and among those now based at Whitchurch was a DH 87 Hornet Moth owned by Mrs P V Wills.

With the change in administration already described, Capt Winters assumed full time responsibility for the airport and its air traffic control and other operational services. The position of Club Secretary now passed to Leonard R Williams, who had been assisting in the administration office for some time, and to both men fell a large share of the responsibility for making arrangements for the four major events of the year – the visit of C W A Scott's British Hospitals Air Pageant on 25March, Empire Air Day on 23 May, the King's Cup Air Race on 10 July (when Whitchurch was a Control Point in an eliminating round), and the Club Garden Party on 5 September. Scott's circus fleet included Airspeed Ferries G-ACFB and G-ABSI, Cierva C.30A Autogiro G-ACUT, BAC Super Drone G-AEED and the red and white chequered Tiger Moth G-ADWG. All four big meetings went well, but

This Mongoose-powered Avro 504N of Heston-based Air Publicity Ltd, was used for banner towing over the Bristol area. Together with 'sky-writing', this was a popular form of advertising in the 1930s. (I Peters via Mac Hawkins)

during the King's Cup race Hendy Heck G-ACTC suffered an undercarriage failure while taxying and Hawk Major G-ADLA over-ran the boundary on landing.

On 5 July the airship *Hindenburg* was seen to the south of the airport and the CFI, the Chairman of the Flying Committee and the Secretary took off in Club aircraft to get a better view. However, the speed and rate of climb of the German airship proved too much for its pursuers and after 35 minutes the three would-be interceptors returned, having got to within two miles of their quarry.

A Tipsy S.2, G-AEOB, was demonstrated to the Club on 11 December, but an arrival on 4 September had been in a very different size and performance category. This was the Vultee V-1A, NR13770 *Lady Peace* flown by Harry Richman and Dick Merrill. The all metal single-engined transport aircraft, normally an eight-seater but its cabin now fitted with long-range fuel tanks, had taken off from Floyd Bennett Field, New York, and landed in a field near Llandeilo in South Wales after an epic 18 hours Atlantic crossing. Low on fuel, the two Americans then flew to Whitchurch, but with no high octane aviation spirit available at the airport they were obliged to make the short hop to Filton, where stocks of the necessary fuel were held, before continuing their journey to Croydon.

The 1920s and 1930s saw a great expansion of Bristol's urban area with the building of something like 36,000 houses. As part of a slum clearance and re-housing plan more than 13,000 of these were built by the Corporation, with many of them on the south side of the city where estates eventually stretched from the Wells Road at Knowle to Bedminster Down. Thus, far sighted as it was in providing the city with a municipal airport, Bristol Corporation at the same time followed a house building programme that progressively encroached upon the airport's boundaries. Initially this was of little consequence, but by the late Thirties housing developments at Knowle West, Filwood Broadway and Hengrove were clearly going to limit expansion of the airport. Already the trend was towards heavier, faster aircraft that required longer take off and landing runs, and while there was no immediate problem at Whitchurch, its days as a potential major airport were already numbered.

CHAPTER FOUR

The Late Thirties

1937

The 1936 fleet of the Bristol and Wessex Aeroplane Club – an Avro Cadet and two BA Swallows – was augmented in January 1937 by another Swallow (G-AESL) With its excellent handling characteristics, low stalling speed and good performance, the Swallow was a popular aircraft and appeared to be living up to its maker's well advertised claim of being 'the safest aircraft built'. Like the first two Swallows, the new aircraft was delivered from Hanworth in a gale, but unlike them it was a Cirrus-powered version.

Compared with the previous year there were few changes in the air services available from Whitchurch in 1937, but the summer Jersey–Exeter schedule of Jersey Airways provided connections with the Railway Air Services Bristol–Plymouth route when Exeter became a request stop from 1 June.

In its first six months of operations from Weston, Western Airways had carried 18,738 passengers, making it one of the busiest provincial airports in the country. Even during the winter months, traffic was heavy on the Weston–Cardiff route, and over the Christmas holidays most of Western's flights were triplicated and run on a half-hourly basis instead of the usual five times daily winter schedule. This augured well for the summer of 1937 and resulted in the installation of Chance airfield lighting to permit night flying. Further, that summer Western Airways augmented its Dragons with two Dragon Rapides. The first was registered G-ADDD, but as with several aircraft operated by Norman Edgar over the years, was not registered in his company's name. Formerly the property of HRH The Prince of Wales and operated by the King's Flight (facts much publicised in due course by Western Airways), G-ADDD was registered in the name of The Channel Trust, Ltd., Weston-super-Mare, on 25 May 1937. A year later it was re-registered to Weston Airport, Ltd., of Brettenhan House, Strand, London WC2, a new company with directors consisting of Whitney S Straight 'and others to be appointed by subscribers', and was not actually registered to Western Airways until 1 November 1938. The second Dragon Rapide, G-ACTU formerly owned by Viscount Forbes, was also registered to The Channel Trust on 14 July 1937. It was re-registered to Weston Airport, Ltd., on 9 April 1938 and, like G-ADDD,

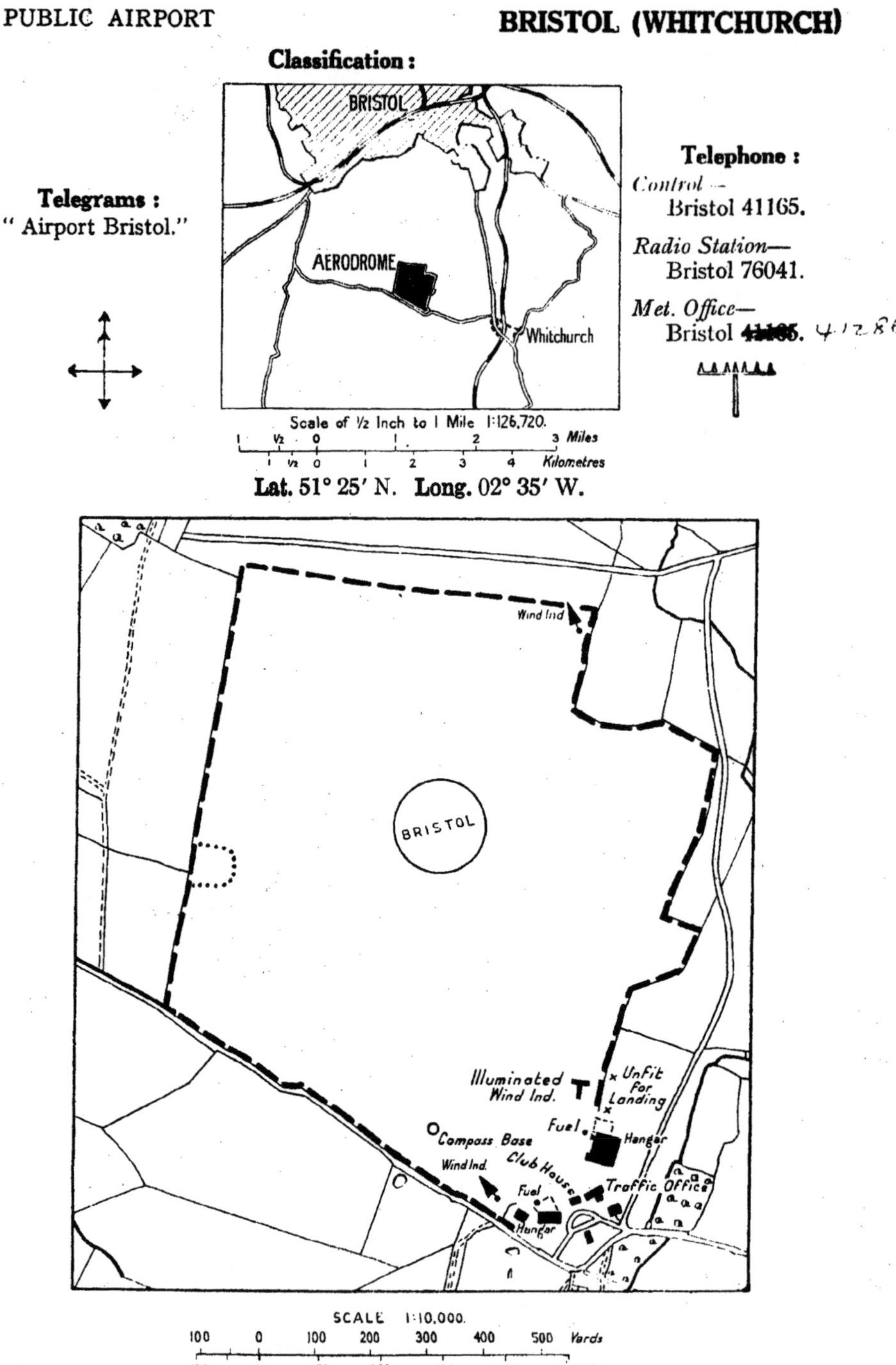

PUBLIC AIRPORT

BRISTOL (WHITCHURCH)

Classification :

Telegrams :
" Airport Bristol."

Telephone :
Control—
Bristol 41165.
Radio Station—
Bristol 76041.
Met. Office—
Bristol ~~41165~~. 41286

Scale of ½ Inch to 1 Mile 1:126,720.

Lat. 51° 25′ N. **Long.** 02° 35′ W.

SCALE 1:10,000.

(38558)—37

Details of Whitchurch, as given in 'The Air Pilot' publication in 1937 (see following two pages). (Author's Collection)

BRISTOL (WHITCHURCH)

1. Controlling Authority.—The Bristol Corporation, Council House, Bristol. (*All communications to* :—The Airport Manager, Bristol Airport, Bristol.)

2. Landing Area

(*a*) *Dimensions.*—

N.—S.	960 yards.
N.E.—S.W.	950 yards.
E.—W.	880 yards.
S.E.—N.W.	900 yards.

(*b*) *Altitude above Mean Sea Level.*—200 feet (61 metres).

(*c*) *Surface Conditions.*—Grass covered.

3. Obstructions Requiring Special Caution

(*a*) *North Side.*—Two radio masts, 70 feet high, 500 yards distant from the N.E. corner of the aerodrome, and 5 radio masts, 70 feet high, 430 yards distant from the N. boundary of the aerodrome.

4. Special Signals.—Nil.

5. Lighting

(1) *Boundary and obstruction lights.*—Red boundary lights (hurricane lamps) delimit the landing area. Red obstruction lights are mounted on the aerodrome buildings in the S.E. corner of the aerodrome and on the radio masts to the N. of the aerodrome.

(2) *Wind indicator.*—An illuminated wind "T" is situated on the E. boundary, approximately 200 yards N. of the aerodrome buildings.

(3) *Floodlight.*—A floodlight, with shadow-bar, is mounted on the roof of the club house in the S.E. corner of the aerodrome.

Note.—The above lights are operated on request only, and two hours' notice is normally required.

6. Facilities for Aircraft

(1) *Refuelling.*—Aviation fuel, oil and fresh water available. Pressure system refuelling pumps are installed.

(2) *Repairs.*—Repairs and aircraft and engine overhauls can be executed at the aerodrome.

BRISTOL (WHITCHURCH)

(3) *Hangars.*—

Number.	Structure.	Net Breadth.	Net Depth.	Door Height.	Door Width.
		ft. in.	ft.	ft. in.	ft. in.
One	Steel and corrugated iron ..	120 0	60	15 0	60 0
One	Steel, corrugated iron and asbestos.	130 6	112	12 0	50 0

(4) *Compass Base.*—Available.

7. Facilities for Personnel

(1) *Transport.*—Bristol railway station, 3 miles. Omnibus service to Bristol. Garages at Bristol. Taxi service from aerodrome.

(2) *Hotels, etc.*—Licensed restaurant at the aerodrome.

8. Local Regulations

(1) When there is no wind, aircraft must land and take off according to the direction indicated by the wind " T " situated on the E. boundary near the S.E. corner of the aerodrome.

(2) Pilots should report to the Aerodrome Control Officer, on arrival and prior to departure, in order that particulars of load, destination, etc., may be recorded. The control office is indicated by a black letter " C " on a yellow background.

9. Customs Arrangements.—Customs facilities are available provided that prior notification that such facilities are required (stating the date and time) is made to the Aerodrome Control. Except in case of emergency, the notice should be sent sufficiently in advance to enable the Customs Authorities to be informed not later than 5 p.m. on the working day (i.e., any week-day other than a public holiday) immediately preceding the day on which facilities are required. All charges and expenses incurred in respect of the attendance of Officers of Customs and Excise must be paid.

A September 1937 view of Whitchurch. Left to right, the buildings are Norman Edgar's showroom, public hangar, Clubhouse (with squash court in front), Traffic Hall (passenger terminal), two 'cottages' at the airport entrance and the Airwork hangar. The Bishopworth–Whitchurch lane crosses the foreground, with the private road to Knowle running diagonally to the right. (Flight)

Although only three miles south of Bristol, the rural setting of the city's airport is very apparent in this 1937 photograph. (Evening World)

Another 1937 view of what was later known as the South Side, Whitchurch, with Dundry Hill in the background. (Author's Collection)

The interior of the Airwork hangar in 1937, with Puss Moth G-ABWZ, three Gipsy Moths, a Miles Hawk, a DH 87A Hornet Moth and Dragon G-ACAO. The latter was owned by Lady Apsley but operated by Western Airways. (Evening World)

was not registered in the name of Western Airways until later that year. Nevertheless, both Rapides (the name shortened from Dragon Rapide by popular usage) were in Western Airways' colours when they came into service in 1937. Like the company's Dragons, the fuselage, engine nacelles and interplane struts of the Rapides were dark blue, with silver wings and tail surfaces; to provide the necessary contrast, registration letters were in dark blue on the wings and silver on the fuselage sides.

Empire Air Day and the annual Garden Party were celebrated in a similar manner to previous years at Whitchurch, but air activity in the Bristol area was showing a marked increase as, with an increasing threat of war, the RAF's Expansion Scheme got under way. Filton was particularly busy and to reduce circuit traffic the Tiger Moths of its resident No 2 Elementary and Reserve Flying Training School (formerly the RAF Reserve Flying School) started using Whitchurch as a relief landing ground. This added significantly to the movements recorded at the airport, where in April the apron was enlarged by Stone & Co of Bristol. Other developments were the opening of a Meteorological Station on 4 May and the acquisition in July of 104 acres from Court Farm to permit extension of the southern and eastern boundaries of the airport. Earlier the Corporation had asked the firm of Norman and Dawbarn to prepare plans for the extension and improvement of the landing area, with new administrative and control buildings on the north side of the airport.

1938

In 1938, with British civil and military aviation continuing to expand, Whitchurch was to assume greater importance as an airport. On 21 February Channel Air Ferries introduced a daily Heston and/or Croydon–Brighton–Isle of Wight–Bournemouth–Bristol–Cardiff service, but later in the year Great Western and Southern Airlines took over some of these sectors. As a result, by late summer GW&SA was flying through Whitchurch on three routes – Liverpool to the Isle of Wight (Ryde) via Manchester, Birmingham, Bristol and Southampton; Shoreham to Bristol via Bournemouth; and Bristol to Penzance via Exeter and Plymouth. In addition, from 23 May Railway Air Services was flying partly in parallel with GW&SA on a Liverpool–Manchester–Birmingham–Gloucester–Bristol–Brighton service, but on 11 September RAS ceased all West and South of England operations. Meanwhile, the Western Airways Weston-Cardiff service continued to gain in popularity and from late July to September certain flights were extended to Swansea. For the 1938 season the company was operating four Dragons, two Rapides and a Puss Moth, and its pilots were C R Cubitt (Chief Pilot), T K Breakell, A L Mortimer, R J T Barrett, C F Almond and G G McLanahan.

There was no Empire Air Day display at Whitchurch in 1938, but the annual Garden Party took place on 28 May and included service

Foster Wickner GM.1 Wicko G-AFAZ of the Bristol and Wesex Aeroplane Club, September 1938. (W K Kilsby)

participation by Wallaces of No 501 (City of Bristol) (Bomber) Squadron and Gloster Gauntlets of No 17 (Fighter) Squadron.

The British aircraft industry suffered a serious loss on 2 August when Capt Frank Barnwell, chief aircraft designer of the Bristol Aeroplane Company, was killed at Whitchurch while flying his Barnwell BSW Mk 1 (G-AFID), an ultra light aircraft of his own design. It was reported that shortly after take off the aircraft appeared to stall and then crashed onto a road adjacent to the airport.

Two important events, the formation of the Civil Air Guard (CAG) and the opening of No 33 Elementary and Reserve Flying Training School (E&RFTS) for the training of RAFVR pilots, were to have a major effect on Whitchurch. The Bristol and Wessex was among the clubs approved by the Air Ministry for CAG trading, the aim being to build up a reserve of pilots for use in time of war. The scheme was due to start on 1 September, but by 18 August a staggering 500 applications had been received by the Club and by 27 October, when the list was closed, the number had reached 700. Nation-wide there were more than 30,000 applicants eager to train for their 'A' Licences at the heavily Government subsidised rate of 5s (25p) an hour. Clubs throughout the country were urgently seeking aircraft and instructors, but luckily the Bristol and Wessex Aeroplane Club had ordered a Foster Wikner GM.1 Wicko earlier in the year. However, although delivery had been expected on 5 August, it was not until mid-October that Wicko G-AFAZ eventually arrived.

Meanwhile, the installation of boundary lighting by GEC was completed in September and work got under way on additional buildings to accommodate No 33 E&RFTS. Operated under contract to the Air Ministry by Chamier, Gilbert and Lodge, Co Ltd, the school opened in December, initially with 12 Tiger Moths. Before long, however, the

The airport's Commer fire engine, supplied and owned by Bristol Corporation with the Avro Cadet of the Bristol and Wessex Club in the background. (M J Tozer Collection)

Dragon II G-ACPX operated through Whitchurch with Railway Air Services in 1935 and with Western Airways from 1936 to 1939. (A J Jackson)

A 1938 Western Airways publicity postcard showing its latest acquisition, Rapide G-ADDD. Seen here in the airline's dark blue and silver colour scheme, this aircraft was formerly owned by the Duke of Windsor and operated by the King's Flight. (Western Airways)

circuit at Whitchurch was reverberating to the more powerful engines of Hawker Audax and Hind Trainers, used for advanced flying instruction, and two Avro Anson Mk Is employed for observer (navigator) and wireless operator training.

One of the most important commercial developments of the year occurred on 18 October when Norman Edgar (Western Airways), Ltd., was renamed Western Airways, Ltd., and taken over by the Straight Corporation. On the same date Norman Edgar's other company, the non-operating Western Air Transport, Ltd., was renamed Straightaway, Ltd. As a result of this re-organisation, in which Norman Edgar became Whitney Straight's commercial supervisor, it was anticipated that Western Airways would expand its operations and enlarge its fleet. By the autumn of 1938 this consisted of three Dragon Is (G-ACAO, G-ACJT and G-ACMJ), two Dragon IIs (G-ACPX and G-AECZ) and three Rapides (G-ACTU, G-ADBV and G-ADDD). One of the latter, G-ADBV, was previously owned by John Dade, a pilot with Olley Air Service, and when it entered service with Western Airways it was still in Olley's black and silver colour scheme. At that time its new owner was listed as Weston Airport, Ltd., but on 1 November the entire fleet was re-registered in the name of Western Airways, Ltd., of 17 Manchester Square, London W1, the address of the Straight Corporation.

1939

For the 1939 season Western Airways, like most other British airlines, was to receive a Government subsidy. It was also operating without direct competition on its routes serving the West Country, a situation brought about by a new licensing system which resulted in RAS's route applications being rejected in favour of similar applications by Western Airways. New routes introduced on 8 May by the West Country airline included a thrice daily Manchester–Birmingham–Bristol–Weston service, and a flight from Weston to Penzance via Barnstaple, from where Lundy and Atlantic Coast Airlines provided a connection to Lundy Island using a Short Scion, a Monospar ST.4 and a DH Moth.

To cope with this rationalisation and route expansion, together with army co-operation contracts to provide 'target' practice for searchlight units in the area, the Western Airways fleet was further enlarged during 1939. A DH 90 Dragonfly (G-AEDH) arrived in February, followed by Percival Q.6 G-AFIX and DH 86B Express G-AETM in April, Rapide G-AFSO in May, another Q.6 (G-AHOM) in June and, finally, Dragon I G-ACLE in September. The entire fleet was repainted in the colour scheme of the Straight Corporation – turquoise (known as Whitney Straight blue) overall with scarlet lettering outlined in white, and scarlet and white striped rudders – but the name Western Airways still appeared on the nose, beneath the stylised 'S' logo of the parent company.

The Weston Aero Club, with F/Lt A L Mortimer as CFI, was also part of the Straight Corporation. It operated a mixed fleet of Hornet Moth, BA Swallow, Miles Hawk Trainer III and, later on, Piper J4 Cub Coupé aircraft, and since 1 October 1938 had been a centre for Civil

In 1939, Rapide G-ADDD was repainted yet again, this time in the colours of the parent Straight Corporation – turquoise overall with red and white rudder stripes. (A J Jackson)

Other Western Airways aircraft operating through Whitchurch in 1939 included DH 84 Dragon II G-ACMJ and those shown below and on page 79. (A J Jackson)

DH 90 Dragonfly G-AEDH. (A J Jackson)

Percival Q.6 G-AFIX. (A J Jackson)

DH 86 Express G-AETM. (A J Jackson)

Air Guard training. Consequently, in addition to its many airline movements, Weston was now a busy training aerodrome and this was exacerbated in July with the formation of No 39 E&RFTS, equipped with Miles Magisters and Hart Trainers for training RAFVR pilots.

At Whitchurch the extra flying brought about by the CAG scheme led the Bristol and Wessex Club to employ two additional instructors, D Kerr Robertson and D A Taylor, and to seek more aircraft. By early summer the CAG Section comprised five Flights, with 25 pupils in each, and the Club's aircraft were in constant use, both by 'Cags' and ordinary members. To cope with this upsurge in activity, another Pobjoy-powered Swallow (G-AEGN) was purchased in April and three new DH 94 Moth Minors were ordered for delivery in July and August.

Earlier, work had started on an extension to the Club House and now contractors were brought in to erect an additional hangar and more huts, workshops and other buildings for No 33 E&RFTS. Upon completion yet more construction work was to start on the north side of the airport as planned from the beginning but yet to be implemented.

Empire Air Day on 20 May was the most impressive yet, with some spectacular demonstrations by the latest service aircraft. Among numerous other items three Fairey Battles dive-bombed a target on the airfield using practice bombs, there was a fly-past by a Short Sunderland flying boat, and a Hawker Hurricane gave a spirited display. However, the most impressive event of the afternoon was the brief appearance of

Cirrus Minor-powered BA Swallow II G-AESL. The hangar in the background, constructed in 1938–39 for No 33 E&RFTS, was occupied during the war by the Bristol Aeroplane Company. (W K Kilsby)

Empire Air Day at Whitchurch, 20 May 1939. The Avro Anson in the foreground (L7046) belonged to the School of Air Navigation and the Hurricane (K1741, coded TM-W) to No 111 Squadron, Northolt. Three Fairey Battles can be seen in the background. (Evening Post)

Two Tiger Moths of No. 33 E&RFTS, Whitchurch, at the 1939 Empire Air Day display. (Evening Post)

Moth Minor G-AFOT and the public hangar (re-painted dark green in 1939). (W K Kilsby)

a Supermarine Spitfire. The RAF's latest fighter made just one high-speed low-level run across the airport, approaching unseen until the very last moment from behind Dundry Hill, and continued northwards to make an equally brief and spectacular appearance at Filton's Air Day.

The first of the three Moth Minors ordered by the Bristol and Wessex Aeroplane Club (G-AFOI) was delivered in early June. A second aircraft (G-AFOU) arrived in mid-August, but the third, registered G-AFOV on 26 August, was never delivered because of the outbreak of war (re-registered VH-ADJ it went instead to Australia).

On 30 August, with war clearly imminent, Whitchurch Airport was declared a Restricted Area and was requisitioned by the Air Ministry. Two days later, on Friday, 1 September, the first of 59 aircraft belonging to Imperial Airways, Ltd., and British Airways, Ltd., were flown in as part of a planned evacuation scheme. The two companies were in the process of merging to become the nationalised British Overseas Airways Corporation (BOAC), but with the outbreak of war the recently approved 'chosen instrument' airline became the basis of National Air Communications (NAC), an organisation formed to carry out essential wartime air transport tasks. With Croydon and Heston airports considered likely targets for air attack, plans had been made to evacuate the embryo headquarters of BOAC to Bristol, with the city's airport becoming the airline's main landplane base. Similarly, the UK-based flying boats of Imperial Airways were moved westwards along the south coast from Hythe, on Southampton Water, to Poole Harbour, Dorset. However, to avoid congestion at Whitchurch, which was now designated 'A' Base, some landplanes were to be based temporarily at Exeter and Coventry (Baginton). Others went to Shoreham, from where many services were subsequently flown to and from the Continent.

To Whitchurch, which until now had rarely seen aircraft bigger than the Rapide, there now came the mighty 'E' and 'F' Class airliners of Imperial Airways, better known as the Armstrong Whitworth AW 27 Ensign and de Havilland DH 91 Albatross. Both had only recently been introduced into service at Croydon and they were very impressive, the Ensign by virtue of its size and the DH 91 because of its beautiful lines. Although named Albatross by its makers, the latter was also widely known as the Frobisher, the name given to the Flagship of its 'F' Class fleet by Imperial Airways.

War was declared on Sunday, 3 September, and with the promulgation of the Air Navigation (Emergency Restriction) Order 1939, followed by the Air Navigation (Restriction in Time of War) Order 1939, all private and club flying was prohibited. At the same time, with the impending call-up of RAFVR pilots for full-time service, the aircraft of

The Club House in 1939, now with an upper storey. Compare with the photo on page 7. (W K Kilsby)

This Handley Page HP 42W (G-AAXC Heracles*) was wrecked during a gale at Whitchurch in 1940. (I Peters via Mac Hawkins)*

DH 91 G-AFDI Frobisher *of Imperial Airways. (British Airways)*

No 33 E&RFTS ceased operating and shortly afterwards were transferred to other RAF flying training schools.

Security was now of great importance and before long barbed wire was introduced to the airport's boundary hedges and fences, buildings were daubed with black and green camouflage paint, and notices prohibiting loitering and the taking of photographs appeared in adjacent roads and lanes. In addition, the private road along the eastern boundary was closed to the public; Air Ministry police posts were built at either end, and for the duration of the war its use was restricted to authorised vehicles only.

Whitchurch was still little more than a large grass field with limited facilities, but it proved just about adequate for the massive fleet which descended upon it that autumn. In general the transfer went quite well, but it was to make a lasting impression on many people, and not only on those directly involved. For local aviation enthusiasts it was a never to be forgotten experience – the latest and biggest aircraft, seen previously only in magazine photographs or as illustrations on cigarette cards, were now everyday realities. Understandably less enthusiastic was the reaction of many actually involved in the move. At very short notice Croydon-based employees were told to pack and prepare to travel by rail or road to an unknown place "somewhere in the West Country". A special train at nearby Waddon Station was loaded with crates of spares and other equipment, and only then did many discover their destination.

Upon arrival at Bristol's Temple Meads Station, staff boarded already

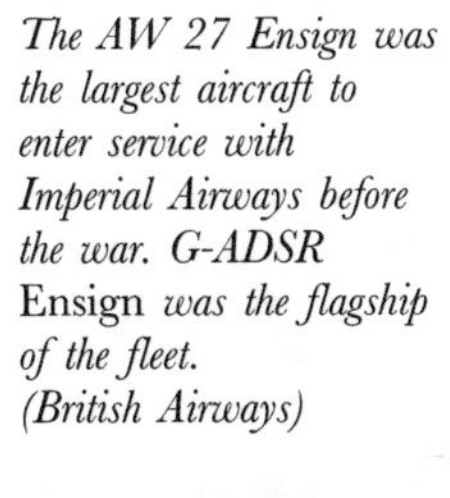

The AW 27 Ensign was the largest aircraft to enter service with Imperial Airways before the war. G-ADSR Ensign *was the flagship of the fleet. (British Airways)*

waiting coaches of Imperial and British Airways which then toured the streets of Bedminster and other districts where, in twos and threes, personnel were to be billeted in various houses. At 7.30 am the next morning, and similarly thereafter, the same coaches were used to pick up staff and take them to Whitchurch, where tents provided temporary accommodation and meals were supplied from field kitchens. Working conditions were primitive, with much of the aircraft maintenance being carried out in the open because of limited hangarage. Until spares, technical records, tools and other equipment arrived, the ability of staff to compromise and improvise was tested to the full, particularly when the coming winter proved to be one of the hardest in living memory. Nevertheless, in the spirit and words of the time, engineering and other staff more than rose to the occasion. Later on, some of the fitters and other engineering staff were posted to Bramcote, where modifications to Ensigns and Lockheed 14s were to be carried out; an engine and propeller overhaul base was also established at Treforest in South Wales, while other staff went to RAF Colerne, near Bath, where, among other tasks, they assisted in assembling US-manufactured Bell Airacobra fighters.

Among the NAC aircraft that arrived at Whitchurch that fateful September (see Appendix IV for full details) were nine Ensigns, including the Flagship of the fleet G-ADSR *Ensign*, and six DH 91s, among them the Flagship G-AFDI *Frobisher*. There were also three Handley

The Lockheed 10A Electra was the first of a new breed of all metal low wing monoplanes to enter service with British Airways Ltd, in 1937. (British Airways)

Airliners of Imperial Airways and British Airways, shortly after their arrival at Whitchurch in September 1939. Seen here are two Ensigns, two Lockheed 14s, a DH 91, an Electra and a Ju 52/3m. (R T Halliwell via P Moss)

Page HP 42s, two Short L.17s and several DH 95 Flamingos. Contrasting strongly with the elderly four-engined HP 42 and L.17 biplanes were the sleek Lockheeds of British Airways – five 10A Electras, two 12As, and seven Model 14s. Also among the early arrivals was a Fokker F.XII and three Junkers Ju 52/3m freighters, but the latter left Whitchurch in October to operate services from Perth to Scandinavia. A variety of smaller aircraft from the internal airlines also flew into Whitchurch, among then some Airspeed Couriers which eventually went to a newly forming British Airways associated organisation known as the Air Transport Auxiliary (ATA).

Upon arrival at Whitchurch one of the first tasks carried out jointly by flying crews and ground staff was the brush application of camouflage paint to the entire fleet. Hastily applied, this led to some rather strange schemes including one by Capt H G Horsey, who painted what were supposed to be white sheep on the brown and green camouflaged upper wing surfaces of an HP 42. Eventually the standard scheme adopted for civil aircraft was Dark Earth and Dark Green upper and side surfaces with natural finish aluminium or silver doped under surfaces. The under surfaces of some aircraft were later painted black, but this was a smooth semi-matt finish, unlike the RAF's soot-like matt black known as Night. Registration letters, which appeared above and

Three Ensigns (one partially camouflaged) and a Ju 52/3m at Whitchurch in September 1939. (R T Halliwell via P Moss)

below the wings and on the fuselage sides, were black, narrowly outlined in silver, and were underlined with horizontal stripes of red, white and blue (red and blue only on the upper wing surface). Some aircraft carried a Union Jack on the nose, where more usually the silver-outlined black Speedbird insignia of Imperial Airways (subsequently adopted by BOAC) appeared. A red, white and blue fin flash was also carried, similar to that seen on RAF aircraft.

Immediately following the outbreak of war NAC flights were started to France in support of the British Expeditionary Force, mainly using Ensigns, DH 91s and HP 42s. Many of these flights were made from Heston, Exeter and Shoreham, the aircraft returning to Whitchurch for maintenance purposes only, as did other machines engaged in flying RAF ground crews from their peacetime bases to new war stations. Daily Heston–Paris flights by DH 91s carried mainly newspapers for the forces, but the more capacious Ensigns moved all manner of freight including foodstuffs and ammunition. At first a few normal fare-paying passengers were carried, but the majority were Government approved or otherwise sponsored by officialdom. Before long travel was restricted to these alone, with most travelling in connection with the war effort or other official business, and a system of priority travel was introduced. In lieu of fares, costs were met by the Government, a situation which prevailed until commercial operations were resumed by BOAC after the war.

Following a grounding at the outbreak of hostilities, several of

Britain's domestic airlines, among them Western Airways, were allowed to resume certain services. Most of these were over-water crossings, but in the case of Western Airways only the Weston–Cardiff service was so approved. Hourly departures each way commenced on 25 November, but following an Air Ministry decision to requisition the company's entire fleet of 18 aircraft, operations were discontinued on 30 March 1940. At that time the Western Airways fleet consisted of four Rapides, five Dragons, one DH 86, three Dragonflies, two Short Scions and two Percival Q.6s. Sadly, during the company's brief reprieve, Dragon G-ACJT crashed on take-off from Weston Airport, killing the pilot, Mr Leslie I Arnott. This occurred on 20 December 1939 and Mr Arnott, an early director of the Company with Norman Edgar, was the sole occupant.

Following earlier problems with their Armstrong Siddeley Tiger IX engines, the Ensigns had been refitted with the more powerful Tiger IXC, but operations during the winter of 1939-40 confirmed that they were still under-powered. Nevertheless, they did some excellent work, but in so doing the weighty aircraft badly rutted the grass surface at Whitchurch. Accordingly, in November 1939 tenders were invited for the construction of a tarmac East-West runway and taxiways linking it to the south-east corner apron and to what was now formally called North Side, where a new Airport Road entrance provided access to hangars and other accommodation intended for BOAC. A taxiway

A Lockheed 14 being brush painted in camouflage colours at Whitchurch by Bob Humphreys (standing on wing), Jack Flinders (sitting on wing), Bert Scovell (kneeling under tailplane) and Jock Mitchell (standing by fin). September 1939. (R G B Wilson)

An Airspeed Courier in RAF markings, as flown from Whitchurch by the ATA in the early days of the war. (L Burch via A J Pitchers)

around the eastern boundary was completed in July 1941, but the 3,048 x 150 ft runway and a taxiway from its western end to the North Side apron were not finished until mid-November. In other directions, a run of 2,870 ft was available for take-offs and landings on the grass towards the north-east or south-west, with 3,060 ft available in a south-easterly/north-westerly direction. However, with Dundry Hill to the south and south-west, rising to 765 ft above sea level within 2½ miles of the airport, extreme caution was necessary when taking off or landing in these directions.

Although the Air Transport Auxiliary was originally formed to operate light aircraft on emergency air transport services, it actually came into existence as a civilian organisation responsible for ferrying aircraft from factories to RAF squadrons or Maintenance Units. British Airways was charged with setting up the new organisation and on 8 September 1939 the first 30 prospective pilots, all of them holders of either 'A' (Private) or 'B' (Commercial) Licences, arrived at Bristol for interviews, medical checks and a flying test in a Tiger Moth. Successful candidates then went on to the RAF's Central Flying School for training prior to their attachment to RAF Ferry Pilot Pools at Hucknall and Filton. Soon, however, an ATA Ferry Pool was established at White Waltham and this was subsequently split into 'A' and 'B' Sections, with 'B' Section taking up residence at Whitchurch.

CHAPTER FIVE

The Early War Years

1940

Although Imperial Airways and British Airways merged fleets on 24 November 1939, they remained part of National Air Communications until 1 April 1940, when BOAC formally came into being. However, the fleet suffered the loss of two HP 42s on 19 March 1940 when G-AAUD *Hanno* and G-AAXC *Heracles* were blown together and damaged beyond repair during a gale at Whitchurch. The fleet was further depleted when two Ensigns were lost during the Battle for France and a third was damaged and reduced to spares shortly afterwards, but throughout this difficult time the civil aircraft and their crews performed magnificently in support of the military.

Earlier, during the German invasion of Belgium and Holland, eight Sabena Belgian Airlines aircraft and six belonging to KLM Royal Dutch Airlines arrived in Britain. The Sabena escapees subsequently departed for service in the Belgian Congo, but the KLM aircraft – a Douglas DC-2 and five DC-3s which arrived at Shoreham from Amsterdam, Lisbon and Naples – were flown to Whitchurch and then on to Heston. This followed discussions between the Air Ministry's Civil Aviation Department and the exiled Dutch Government that resulted in the KLM machines operating under charter to BOAC. Accordingly, although re-registered in the UK and repainted in BOAC-style camouflage, all six aircraft – then some of the most modern in Europe – proudly retained their Dutch names (see Appendix VI).

Another refugee airliner at Whitchurch that summer was the four-engined Focke Wulf FW 200B Condor OY-DAM *Dania* of DDL Danish Airlines. It arrived in the bright orange finish that proclaimed, in vain, its neutrality, but was quickly camouflaged, re-registered G-AGAY and renamed *Wolf*. Later, with the intention of using it to fly the Royal Family to Canada in the event of a German invasion, the Condor was flown to the Cunliffe-Owen factory at Southampton (Eastleigh), where additional fuel tanks were installed to extend its already long range. Overhauled and repainted in RAF markings as DX177, it then went to the ATA at White Waltham, where it was damaged beyond repair in a landing accident on 12 July 1941.

NAC was disbanded on 22 June, following the French collapse, and in its place came an organisation called Associated Airways Joint

Dummy 'hedgerows' of cinders, intended to give the landing area a field pattern, failed to fool the Germans, as this 1940 Luftwaffe reconnaissance photo of Whitchurch reveals. German annotations show: (A) Target No. GB 10 26, the airport itself; (B) Target GB 17 9, the wireless communications and D/F Stations; and (C) the AA gunsite to the east of the airport. (Author's Collection)

Committee (AAJC). Principally consisting of small domestic airlines, AAJC was formed to operate essential internal services, thus leaving BOAC free to concentrate on international routes. From the UK these included a Whitchurch–Lisbon service which usually routed via Heston to load and unload passengers. Inaugurated on 6 June by the DH 91 G-AFDL *Fingal*, this service was soon disrupted by the German occupation of Western France, but from bases in the Middle East, South Africa and elsewhere, BOAC continued to operate many of the pre-war Empire routes of Imperial Airways, using a mixed fleet of landplanes and flying boats.

With the direct UK–Lisbon route made hazardous by the German occupation of France, it became necessary to make a long detour, heading out to the 10° West meridian before turning south to cross the Bay of Biscay. And here the excellent range/payload characteristics of the DC-3 made it particularly suitable as a replacement for the DH 91. Accordingly, a trial service was flown by KLM on 26 July 1940 and from 10 August the Dutch airline assumed full responsibility for the route. Operating under the charter arrangement with BOAC, KLM was to make four flights a week with DC-3s and a fifth with the DC-2. Services were flown from their Heston base, but on 20 September the KLM fleet and ground organisation re-located to Whitchurch. As before, however, passengers were to join at Heston and it was here, on 21 September while operating the first service to originate from Whitchurch, that DC-3 G-AGBC was written off while attempting to land in fog. The aircraft, flown by Capt Quirinus Tepas, was damaged beyond repair when it struck one of the anti-invasion poles erected to prevent landings by German troop-carrying transport aircraft and gliders, but there were no passengers on board and no crew members were injured. The remaining aircraft, flown by Dutch crews and maintained by Dutch and British mechanics, went on to establish a remarkable record on what was a very difficult and dangerous route.

By September 1940 the ATA's 'B' Section at Whitchurch had become a Ferry Pool in its own right. Initially operating from a hut on the South Side with 12 pilots, it rapidly grew to become No 2 Ferry Pool (White Waltham being No 1) and moved to larger premises on the North Side of the airport. Several well known pilots served with the unit including Norman Edgar, the founder of Western Airways, and Capt O P Jones, who was seconded from BOAC/Imperial Airways to become the Pool's first commander. Later transferred back to BOAC, he was succeeded by Commander Leonard M Leaver, formerly a member of the Airport Management Committee and a director of the Bristol and Wessex Aeroplane Club. He was to serve as the Pool's commanding officer for the next four years, his second-in-command being Capt George L Pine, the founder of Pine's Airways which in happier times carried out pleasure flights from the seafront at Porthcawl.

No 2 Ferry Pool was primarily concerned with the delivery of Blenheims, Beauforts and Beaufighters from Filton, Hurricanes built by Gloster Aircraft at Hucclecote, Spitfires and Whirlwinds produced by Westland Aircraft at Yeovil, various heavy bombers from the RAF Maintenance Unit at St Athan, near Barry, and, later on, Beaufighters from Weston-super-Mare. Many other deliveries, covering a wide range of aircraft, also came its way, and for training and checking purposes a Fairey Battle Trainer was allocated to the Pool. For use as 'taxi' aircraft, for the collection and general positioning of its pilots, the Pool was also allocated an Airspeed Courier, a DH 90 Dragonfly and a Piper J4 Cub Coupé, but the taxi fleet was soon standardised on the Avro Anson Mk I, modified to carry ten passengers. From May 1942 extensive use was also made of the luxurious four-seat Fairchild 24W-41 Argus. Maintenance of the taxi fleet, and servicing the many different types in transit, was the responsibility of ground staff mainly seconded from, or recruited by, British Airways/BOAC.

At no time were RAF squadrons stationed at Whitchurch (now also known by the code letters 'JP') so it played no direct part in the Battle of Britain. Nevertheless, it was an extremely busy time for the airport with, among other types, many Spitfires and Hurricanes passing through in the hands of ATA pilots.

Throughout that summer and autumn the threat of invasion was very real and at dusk, following the last movement of the day, numerous old cars were scattered over the landing area to prevent possible landings by German troop-carrying gliders or transport aircraft. Guard and aerodrome defence duties were initially undertaken by a small detachment of soldiers, whose tented camp was in an orchard near the South Side entrance, but from mid-1940 these duties passed to the Air Ministry Constabulary and a Home Guard unit formed by BOAC staff. Concrete pill boxes also appeared at strategic points on and around the airport and although there was no specific defence against air attack, a Heavy Anti-Aircraft battery of AA Command, Royal Artillery, occupied a site in Ridgeway Lane, Whitchurch. In addition, from the earliest days of the war light AA machine guns had been positioned on several nearby searchlight and barrage balloon sites and later on there was a Z-Rocket battery on the Bishopsworth or west side of the airport, manned by members of the Home Guard.

Despite all the flying activity at Whitchurch, incidents and accidents were comparatively few. Barrage balloons, of which there were 96 in the Bristol area in 1940, were a great hazard at times, especially in conditions of low cloud and poor visibility, but no collisions were reported. However, aircraft being ferried by the ATA occasionally landed with engine or undercarriage trouble and a few belly landings occurred. Several aircraft, including a Wellington and an Anson, also overran on landing and on 16 October two out of three Hurricanes belonging to No 504 Squadron were damaged while attempting to land in bad weather. 'Scrambled' from Filton in an unsuccessful attempt to intercept an enemy aircraft, they were unable to return to base because of low cloud and rain, but their leader succeeded in finding Whitchurch, where one Hurricane landed safely, another went up onto its nose after touch-down and the third, R4178 flown by Pilot Officer 'Reggie'

Tongue, a well known racing driver, finished up in a pond just outside the southern boundary hedge.

With the autumn came an unwanted depletion of the BOAC fleet. On 6 October 1940 the DH 91 G-AFDL *Fingal* was written off at Pucklechurch, near Bristol, while on a flight from Whitchurch to Bramcote. Shortly after take-off all four engines failed, apparently because of a faulty cross-feed cock in the fuel system, and with little height in hand Capt E White was forced to make an emergency landing, striking part of a cottage in the process. *Fingal* was damaged beyond repair, but all three crew and nine passengers survived. A few days later an arson attack by a disgruntled former employee resulted in the destruction of *Frobisher*, the Flagship of the fleet, followed shortly afterwards by a repeat performance that resulted in fire damage to *Faraday* one of two former special long-range versions of the Albatross. Earlier, on 9 September, the Corporation had lost one of its two Short L.17s when *Scylla* was wrecked in a gale in Scotland. Outdated and increasingly difficult to maintain, the surviving L.17 *Syrinx* was scrapped.

Despite the many problems facing it, the airline maintained services at a good level, as revealed by traffic figures for October. Typically, that month 40 services were flown to and from Lisbon; on outward flights 154 passengers were carried, with 6,408 kgs of mail and 3,452 kgs of freight. Figures for inward flights were 118 passengers, 5,302 kgs of mail and 4,134 kgs of freight. However, the reduction in the size of the BOAC fleet continued, both at home and overseas, and more losses occurred on 24 November when Ensign G-ADTC *Endymion* and the KLM DC-3 G-AGBI *Wulp* were destroyed by incendiary bombs during a heavy night Blitz on Bristol. In addition, splinters and debris damaged Ensigns G-ADSV, G-ADSY and G-ADTB, Condor G-AGAY and DC-3 G-AGBB, but all were repaired and soon returned to service. Nevertheless, the fall of France had placed Bristol right in the front line and as an important port and vital centre of the aircraft industry it suffered badly. Whitchurch was constantly under threat and numerous bombs fell on and around the landing area, but in spite of this operations continued without serious interruption.

Around this time BOAC also came under threat from another quarter. This was an attempt by the Bristol Aeroplane Company, supported by the Ministry of Aircraft Production, to oust the Corporation from Whitchurch. The BAC wanted the airport in its entirety for use as a Beaufighter 'shadow' factory, but the suggestion that BOAC should move to RAF Colerne, near Bath, was violently and successfully opposed. However, the BAC did eventually occupy much of the South Side, initially for assembling and then storing Beaufighter Mk II airframes awaiting deliveries of Rolls-Royce Merlin engines. Later on the company established a major engine overhaul depot on the same side of the airport and also occupied a hangar on the North Side.

1941

On 22 May 1941 Foynes, on the River Shannon in neutral Eire, became the northern terminus of BOAC's West African (Lagos) flying boat service. Foynes was already used by flying boats of Pan American Airways, whose transatlantic flights connected with a BOAC shuttle service to Poole Harbour, and with the arrival of some new Boeing 314As, BOAC was to join Pan American on the route. American Export Airlines also planned to use Foynes and the overall increase in traffic called for more capacity on the UK-Eire route. As a result it was decided to augment and finally replace the Foynes–Poole Harbour flying boat service with a landplane shuttle. Accordingly, on 4 July BOAC commenced a Whitchurch–Dublin service with DH 91s, but before long the service was significantly improved when an airport at Foynes (Rineanna) became available. Better known as Shannon, this became a major terminal for transatlantic landplane flights in the immediate post-war period.

In August 1941 the first of the nine surviving Ensigns was flown to Bramcote to be re-engined yet again. This time, in a bid to significantly improve both performance and reliability, the fleet was to be fitted with 1,100 hp Wright Cyclone GR-1820-G102As, with which motors they were known as Ensign Mk IIs. The modification programme continued into 1942 with the aircraft returning to Whitchurch after conversion, but the intention was to base them in Cairo for trans-African operations. In the meantime they flew services from Whitchurch, the first re-engined Ensign carrying out several flights to Foynes in September.

In due course the Ensigns departed for Cairo, one at a time and

The 'E' Class flagship Ensign, *after conversion to Mk II standard with four Wright Cyclone engines. (A J Pitchers)*

A Lockheed 14 undergoing maintenance in 1941. (A J Pitchers)

spread over several months. En route they landed at Portreath to uplift maximum fuel for the long 10° West crossing of the Bay of Biscay, but G-AFZU *Everest*, one of the last Ensigns to be delivered, had the misfortune to encounter a Heinkel He 111 shortly after leaving the English coast. Although the He 111 fired only a single burst it managed to damage both the airliner's main spar and its hydraulic system. The Ensign, with Capt A P Flowerday in command, was put into a steep dive in a bid to escape and in so doing reached an incredibly high speed for the normally sedate airliner. Levelling out a few feet above the sea the Ensign made good its escape and returned to base, where use of the emergency hand pump was necessary to lower its undercarriage. Following repairs *Everest* again left for Africa where it joined other Ensigns operating services from Khartoum to Lagos and Asmara. The Ensigns also took over the Cairo–Calcutta sector of the UK-Australia route, but it was not until January 1943 that *Egeria*, the last aircraft to be re-engined, departed Whitchurch. Meanwhile, on 12 October 1941 a regular Whitchurch–Cairo service was started, routing via Lisbon and Gibraltar. The Corporation also commenced a service from Gibraltar to Malta, using both landplanes and flying boats, and this was probably the most hazardous sector of all those flown by BOAC in wartime. With a constant high level of German air activity it could only be flown under cover of darkness, but even then the beleaguered island was usually under attack.

From the summer of 1940 until mid-1941, when Russia was invaded by Germany, Britain stood alone, virtually isolated from the rest of the world. With her sea approaches constantly threatened by German U-boats, air transport came into its own. Communications with friendly countries, and particularly with the USA and the British

A KLM DC-3 ready to depart Whitchurch for Lisbon. (Author's Collection)

Commonwealth, were absolutely vital, as were contacts with neutral countries in connection with Prisoner of War mail and other matters. And in all of this, BOAC was indispensable. Throughout the war it performed magnificently, but at no time were its landplane and flying boat services more valuable than during the bleak 1940-1941 period, with Whitchurch playing its part in full as one of Britain's few gateways to the free world. However, the rôle played by Whitchurch was never revealed in wartime. For security reasons it was always referred to as 'a West Country airport' as was the case in March 1941 when Mr J G Winant, the American Ambassador, arrived from the USA by way of Lisbon and an onward flight to Britain in a KLM DC-3.

In the two years following the outbreak of war BOAC lost about 20 aircraft, mainly due to accidents and enemy action, and gained about 50. But although enlarged, the Corporation's fleet was still inadequate for its extensive route network and the government was therefore asked to provide additional, more modern aircraft. Consequently, nine

Commander Leonard Leaver, the commanding officer of No. 2 Ferry Pool, Whitchurch, for four years. (L Burch via A J Pitchers)

Lockheed Lodestars were obtained from the USA, mainly for services within Africa. Three ex-RAF Lockheed Hudsons were also added to the BOAC fleet, as were four DH 95 Flamingos that had been ordered before the war but not delivered. More Lodestars followed and upon assuming responsibility for the Atlantic Return Ferry Service on 24 September 1941, BOAC added six more Consolidated LB.30 Liberators to one it already possessed, operating them between Montreal and Prestwick and, later on, to Cairo from Lyneham and Hurn. By the end of 1941, with some of its older overseas-based aircraft scrapped and others transferred to the RAF, the Corporation was operating 63 aircraft (27 flying boats and 36 landplanes), excluding the six-strong KLM fleet. The exact number based at Whitchurch at that time is not known, but in addition to the KLM aircraft it included six Ensigns, three DH 91s and the recently acquired prototype Curtiss Wright CW-20.

The CW-20, the forerunner of the USAAF's C-46 Commando, was then the world's largest twin-engined aircraft. Formerly registered NX19436, the CW-20 went to the USAAF as a cargo aircraft (serial number 41-21041), but when purchased by BOAC it was fitted with 24 passenger seats and long-range tanks were installed. On 12 November 1941 the CW-20, now registered G-AGDI and named *St Louis,* was flown across the Atlantic to Prestwick and then on to Whitchurch by Capt A C P Johnstone. After a period of crew training, it operated services to Gibraltar and Shannon and from May 1942 was also used on the Gibraltar–Malta night run.

In some respects the CW-20 was well ahead of its time, but this resulted in a number of maintenance problems. In particular its complex electrical system required much attention, but even ground running its engines was not without incident. Bernard Morey, then an 'improver' or apprentice fitter with BOAC Engineering recalls: "Invariably the starboard engine of the CW-20 would catch fire on start up, and the usual flap would start. Flames belting out of the exhaust tail pipe, probably due to over-priming, necessitated prompt action on the part of the ground crew". With further reference to its mighty 1,600 hp Wright Cyclone 586 series engines Bernard Morey recalls: "When the prevailing south-west wind was blowing I could hear them at full throttle from my home eight miles away, the tip speed of the big diameter propellers creating a deafening noise".

In October 1943, with the arrival of more suitable aircraft, the *St Louis* was taken out of service and on 7 January 1944 it was flown to Filton and handed over to the Bristol Aeroplane Company. Subsequently, after a detailed examination by BAC engineers, some of its undoubtedly advanced features were adopted for the post-war airliner project that eventually materialised as the Bristol Brabazon. The *St Louis* flew for the last time on 1 September 1944 and early in December its wings were removed to start a breaking-up process that was not completed until March 1945.

1942

There was nothing apparently unusual about the KLM DC-3 that arrived at Whitchurch from Lisbon on Friday, 20 February 1942, but if anything could be described as 'the start of something big', then this was it. Among the passengers were seven US Army Air Force staff officers, wearing civilian clothes but here to prepare the way for the mightiest strategic bomber arm ever assembled – the US Eighth Air Force. Led by Brigadier General Ira C Eaker, the group continued without delay to London and subsequently set in motion plans for the USAAF to join RAF Bomber Command in the joint air offensive against Germany.

A less warlike event that February was a visit to Whitchurch by HRH The Duke of Kent. Met by Capt L P Winters and representatives of the Air Ministry and BOAC, the Duke was introduced to Mr W D van Os, Technical Manager of KLM, and some of his engineering staff. He also met Capt T von Weyhrosher and was shown around one of the company's DC-3s before going on to inspect No 2 Ferry Pool, where he spoke with a number of ATA pilots.

During April and May 1942 BOAC received some Armstrong Whitworth Whitley Mk V heavy bombers for use as freighters but, following conversion, proving flights from Whitchurch to West Africa revealed that they were not really suitable for operation in hot climates. Nevertheless 13 aircraft, registered G-AGCF to G-AGCK, G-AGDU, G-AGDX to G-AGDZ and G-AGEA to G-AGEC, went into service, flying from Whitchurch to Lagos, Gibraltar and occasionally Shannon. They also operated between Leuchars and Stockholm and were used on the extremely hazardous night run between Gibraltar and Malta until replaced by more suitable Hudsons in August 1942. Although not equipped to carry passengers, Whitleys with mattresses on their floors in lieu of seats sometimes carried RAF aircrew personnel from

From May 1942 the Fairchild 24W-41 Argus Mk I, later joined by the more powerful Mk II, was used by the ATA as a four-seat taxi aircraft. (L Burch via A J Pitchers)

An Armstrong Whitworth Whitley Mk V transport, used by BOAC in 1942. (BA/Adrian Meredith Photography)

Whitchurch to Gibraltar, but from early 1943 until the end of the year, when they were returned to the RAF, the converted bombers were used mainly on Leuchars–Stockholm services. One aircraft, G-AGDY, was damaged at Portreath on 20 September 1942, but only one Whitley was lost while in service with BOAC. This was G-AGCI, which crashed into the sea off Gibraltar on 26 September 1942 with the loss of Capt C G K Browne, Second Officer S D J Curnock, Navigating Officer P R Dean and Radio Officer R S Mallett.

Aircraft of RAF units were frequent visitors to Whitchurch, the most regular being Airspeed Oxfords and Miles Masters from nearby Lulsgate Bottom, the Flying Training Command station destined one day to become Bristol Airport in place of Whitchurch. But unlike most RAF visitors to Whitchurch, a new North Side resident from 30 July 1942 was an aircraft reminiscent of pre-war days. This was a DH 82A Tiger Moth II (BB857, formerly G-ADOX), issued to the Bristol University Air Squadron to give pre-entry air experience to students intent on joining the RAF.

During October 1942 the airport received another Royal visit, this time by Her Majesty Queen Mary, the Queen Mother, following which it was officially announced that she had *"visited the main headquarters of BOAC in the West Country and Royal Dutch Air Lines (KLM). Her Majesty inspected the various departments of the Corporation and showed a lively interest in British war transport. She was introduced to a number of Corporation and KLM staff members and made a thorough inspection of one of KLM's DC-3s".*

Almost every type of landplane and amphibian used by the RAF and Fleet Air Arm passed through Whitchurch in the hands of ATA pilots, including rarities like the Mohawk, Airacobra and Sea Otter. Early each morning, before small parties of men and women ferry pilots boarded them, the Argus and Anson taxi aircraft were pre-flight checked and their engines run-up by mechanics. They then departed to various destinations, but came and went again throughout the day, collecting and delivering ferry pilots until a final return to base at dusk. And while all this was going on a succession of service aircraft passed through, en route to or from factories, RAF units or other Ferry Pools, making Whitchurch a paradise for aircraft enthusiasts who chose to disregard the 'No Loitering' signs in Whitchurch Lane and elsewhere around the airport perimeter. The objects of their attention ranged in size from the Taylorcraft Auster to the Stirling and Lancaster, but some types were still on the secret list and not so readily identified. They included, at various times, the Beaufighter, Whirlwind, Typhoon, Mosquito, Tempest, Firefly, Barracuda and Warwick.

Secret variants of already well known types were also seen from time to time, including Whitley VIIs bristling with highly secret Air–Surface Vessel radar antennae, Beaufighter VIs with 'thimble' noses containing Airborne Interception (AI) radar, and Halifax IIIs with under-fuselage H2S radar navigation 'blisters'. And although it did not land, even a Gloster Meteor, the RAF's first operational jet fighter, was once seen at very close quarters during a low level 'beat-up' of the ATA Operations Office. Some of the most spectacular beat-ups, however, were those performed regularly by BAC test pilots in the Merlin-powered Beaufighter IIs that were assembled in the South Side Flight Shed.

The Curtiss CW-20 G-AGDI St Louis *at Whitchurch, April 1942. (A J Pitchers)*

Engineering staff of No. 2 Ferry Pool, Whitchurch. (L. Burch via A J Pitchers)

Capt O P Jones (centre front), the first commander of No 2 Ferry Pool, with a group of ATA and BOAC pilots at Whitchurch. (L Burch via A J Pitchers)

Like most aviation organisations, the ATA was not without its share of amusing and enterprising individuals. One such character was First Officer David Coopper who, between two periods at Whitchurch, was stationed at Belfast for the main purpose of ferrying Stirlings from the Short Brothers factory to RAF Maintenance Units in the Midlands. When posted back to Whitchurch from Belfast David Coopper decided to 'move house' by air, making unofficial use of a Stirling to do so. Obtaining a 'removal' van from the MT Section at Belfast and arranging a ferry flight to England presented no problems, but when the day came the Stirling happened to be one classed 'NEA' – 'not entirely airworthy' and cleared for one landing only. Consequently, routing to its intended destination in the Midlands with an unauthorised interim landing at Whitchurch presented an additional problem, but a resourceful David Coopper hoped to avoid trouble by landing at Whitchurch late in the day, after Commander Leaver, the Pool's commanding officer, had gone home. This was successfully accomplished, the Stirling was unloaded and once again the local MT Section willingly provided a van to transport his belongings, which included a large collection of antiques, to his home in Clifton. As expected, questions were asked the next day and despite some prior collusion between Coopper and the Whitchurch Meteorological Office, Commander Leaver was not altogether satisfied that the landing at Whitchurch had been due to bad weather. However, there were no serious repercussions for Coopper, who said: "At least I can probably claim to be the only pilot ever to move house by Stirling!".

From 15 October 1942 KLM extended its Whitchurch–Lisbon service with two flights each week continuing to Gibraltar. However, the Battle of the Atlantic was increasing in intensity and to counter RAF Coastal Command's anti-submarine aircraft the Luftwaffe was now flying long-range fighter patrols far out over the Bay of Biscay and the Western Approaches. This clearly posed a threat to civil aircraft flying the 10° West route (1,000 miles over the sea, but all of it within range of enemy aircraft) and the anticipated danger became reality on 15 November when DC-3 G-AGBB *Ibis* was attacked over the Bay by a lone German aircraft. Fortunately, the KLM DC-3 was able to escape in cloud, having sustained only minor damage.

Despite the introduction of various new services from Whitchurch, the most frequently flown at the end of 1942 were still those to Lisbon and Foynes, respectively operated mainly by DC-3s of KLM and DH 91s of BOAC. Passengers started and finished their journeys at the Grand Hotel, Bristol, where they were checked-in and where the hotel lounge served as a waiting room It was here that passengers took leave of friends or next-of-kin before boarding the airport bus. Customs, immigration and security formalities were completed upon arrival at Whitchurch, where the airside doors of the South Side passenger building provided immediate access to aircraft parked on the apron in front of the control tower.

CHAPTER SIX

Victory in Europe

1943

Until now BOAC, like Imperial Airways before it, had employed only Stewards as cabin staff, but in 1943 the Corporation recruited its first five Stewardesses. Upon completion of their training they were to be employed mainly on services to Lisbon and Foynes, routes on which new aircraft were also soon to appear. This occurred in March, when BOAC's long quest for new transport aircraft was partially satisfied when six Douglas C-47 Dakota Mk Is were diverted to the Corporation from a batch supplied to the RAF under the Lend-Lease agreement. Although the RAF name 'Dakota' was then unfamiliar, the aircraft themselves were not, for they were military versions of the well known DC-3, with strengthened cabin floors and large double entry doors. The new aircraft (powered by two 1,200 hp Pratt and Whitney Twin Wasp

Capt H H 'Bow' Perry of BOAC in the control buidling at Whitchurch prior to take off. (IWM)

This Avro Anson Mk I (N4877) was one of many based at Whitchurch with No 2 Ferry Pool. The gun turret was later removed from most ATA Ansons. (A J Pitchers)

R-1830-92 engines) could accommodate up to 32 passengers, but 21 was the norm. Flexibility was achieved by easily removable passenger seats, which also facilitated quick conversion to an all-freight or mixed freight/passenger configuration. By the end of the year the six Mk Is, registered G-AGFX to G-AGGB and G-AGGI, were joined by 14 of an eventual fleet of 30 improved C-47A Dakota Mk IIIs, with registrations in the range G-AGHE to G-AGJZ. Later on, the six Mk Is were converted to Mk III standard with, among other things, their 12-volt electrical systems replaced by the 24-volt electrics of the later version.

On 19 April 1943 the KLM DC-3 *Ibis* had a second brush with the enemy. This time, when 3½ hours out from Whitchurch en route to Lisbon, it was attacked by several Messerschmitt Bf 110 long-range fighters. Capt D Parmentier dived *Ibis* to sea level and managed to escape with only a punctured fuel tank, which fortunately was empty. Passengers on board included the British Assistant Air Attaché to Portugal and four Irish novice priests, but no one was hurt.

BOAC began operating Dakotas on the Whitchurch–Lisbon service on 11 May, the inaugural flight being carried out by G-AGGI, but on 1 June KLM's DC-3 *Ibis* had yet another encounter with the enemy. And this time it was a case of third time unlucky. That day Capt Quirinus Tepas, OBE, who had been with KLM since 1925 and was the company's Chief Pilot, departed Lisbon's Portella Airport at 0730 GMT. The flight progressed normally for three hours but at 1030 (1230 local time in Britain) a radio message from Ibis to 'GKH' (then the

Mechanics at work on a BOAC Dakota at Whitchurch in 1943. The Speedbird insignia of Imperial Airways was successively adopted by BOAC and today's British Airways, but was discarded in 1982. However, 'Speedbird' remains the airline's radio callsign. (IWM)

W/T call-sign for Whitchurch) indicated that it was being attacked by several aircraft. Whitchurch responded with a request for more details, but nothing further was heard. The DC-3 had been intercepted by a patrol of eight Ju 88C-6s of V./KG 40, a long-range fighter *Gruppe* operating from Bordeaux-Merignac and Kerlin-Bastard, and the result was a foregone conclusion. Four crew members – co-pilot Capt D de Koning, Radio Operator C van Brugge and Flight Engineer E Rozevink, in addition to Capt Tepas – and 13 passengers were lost, among them two children and Leslie Howard, the well known actor.

Following this disaster night flights were introduced, with KLM temporarily withdrawing from the route as its aircraft were not equipped with flame-damping exhaust shrouds and astro navigation observation domes. Consequently, until the KLM aircraft were equipped with these essential night flying items, BOAC increased its own Lisbon flights to four per week, operating by night in both directions. Following KLM practice, refuelling stops were made when necessary at Oporto on northbound flights, and at either Chivenor, Portreath or St Mawgan when southbound. Departures from Lisbon were normally timed to ensure arrival at Whitchurch at daybreak, as, with no approach lights or proper flarepath, night landings on the short east-west runway, particularly in bad weather, were clearly undesirable.

Despite all the difficulties associated with the operation, KLM's record on the Whitchurch–Lisbon service was quite remarkable. In the

From 1941 to 1943 some BOAC aircraft carried the Union flag in place of the Speedbird, as seen on this Dakota at Whitchurch with the legendary Capt O P Jones. (IWM)

A dawn scene at Whitchurch, with ground staff and a crew car awaiting the arrival of a flight from Lisbon. A DH 91 can be seen in the background. (IWM)

Running-up the engines of DC-3 Zilverreiger *outside KLM's North Side hangar. (IWM)*

The KLM DC-2 Edelvalk, *seen here with its camouflage paint removed from the fin and rudder. (A J Jackson)*

DC-3 Buizerd *of KLM with its cowlings removed, undergoing engine runs at Whitchurch after maintenance. Several Dakotas and a DH 91 of BOAC can be seen on the North Side parking area. (IWM)*

The wireless (D/F) operator at work in the radio room of the control tower at Whitchurch, June 1943. (Air Ministry)

three years to 26 July 1943 a total of 1,622 flights were completed, with a regularity of more than 94 per cent, and nearly 10,000 passengers were carried.

During the summer of 1943 a Dakota service to Fez, North Morocco, was introduced, with a destination change to Rabat in early September. Temporarily Lyneham was used for departures, with the return flights terminating at Whitchurch, which again became the departure airport from 31 December.

Strong winds across the single runway at Whitchurch were not normally a problem because its good, well-drained grass area allowed landings to be made into wind, except during very wet periods in the winter. The strongest winds were often those associated with south-westerly gales and it was not unusual, therefore, to see Dakotas coming in low over the Knowle Park and Knowle West housing estates, their navigation lights switched on in the first light of a windy dawn, to touch down on the North Side tarmac and complete their landing run on the grass. However, diversion facilities were always available at Lyneham, Chivenor, St Mawgan and Portreath. Nearby Lulsgate Bottom was also a useful diversion airfield when Whitchurch was shrouded in early morning mist or radiation fog. In such conditions Lulsgate, being some 600-ft above sea level, was usually clear while fog filled the valleys around it, but frontal weather often made landing at Lulsgate impossible because of cloud on the surface.

In 1943, when he was aged 51, Capt H H 'Bow' Perry was BOAC's oldest captain. A World War One pilot, he is seen here on the South Side apron at Whitchurch, with a Dakota in the background. (BOAC)

A typical departure sequence from Whitchurch in June 1943. The DH 91 Fortuna *has been towed to the South Side apron in readiness for a trip to Shannon. (IWM)*

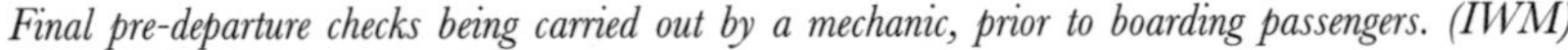

Final pre-departure checks being carried out by a mechanic, prior to boarding passengers. (IWM)

Passengers leave the Departure Hall to board Fortuna, *with a Stewardess waiting to greet them. The windows of the DH 91's cabin have been covered to prevent passengers seeing and perhaps photographing security sensitive areas on the ground. (IWM)*

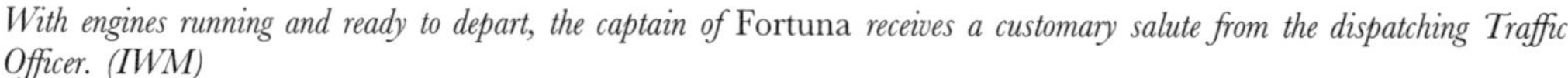

With engines running and ready to depart, the captain of Fortuna *receives a customary salute from the dispatching Traffic Officer. (IWM)*

ATA Ansons in RAF markings were among the most frequently seen aircraft at Whitchurch, but in the summer of 1943 20 Anson Mk Is in BOAC markings arrived. Their stay was short, however, because they were actually RAF aircraft bound for the Middle East. Their registrations (G-AGGJ to G-AGHD) and other civilian markings were no more than a ruse that permitted them to refuel in neutral Portugal. Had they arrived at Lisbon in military markings, they and their crews would have been interned in accordance with International Law. As BOAC aircraft, flown by 'civilian' crews, all went according to plan and they duly arrived at Aboukir and Almaza by way of Lisbon and Takoradi.

The DH 91s had continued to shuttle between Whitchurch and Shannon but the last service operated by this type took place on 6 July 1943. Shortly before landing at Shannon that day, Capt G P Moss was forced to crash-land G-AFDK *Fortuna* on a mud flat when one of its flaps broke away and badly damaged the tail. *Fortuna* was totally wrecked, but amazingly there were no crew injuries and of the eight passengers on board – four directors and four senior officials of BOAC – only one was slightly hurt. Pending an inquiry into what appeared to be a structural failure, the remaining two DH 91s, *Falcon* and *Fiona*, were grounded at Whitchurch and in September they were scrapped.

Fortunately, more Dakotas with trained crews were now available to replace the DH 91s and from 4 August BOAC resumed a twice weekly Whitchurch–Gibraltar service. Further, from 24 October a weekly Whitchurch–Madrid–Lisbon service was started, followed a month later by a service to Algiers. Flying Whitchurch–St Mawgan (for a fuel top-

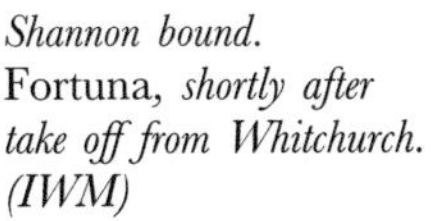

Shannon bound. Fortuna, *shortly after take off from Whitchurch. (IWM)*

A Ford V8 Mobile Canteen of BOAC's Catering Branch provides a welcome tea break for crews at Whitchurch in the summer of 1943. (IWM)

A BOAC Traffic Officer supervises the loading of what appears to be an Ensign tyre into a Dakota III at Whitchurch in 1943. (IWM)

Two Navigating Officers and two Radio Officers play 'shove ha'penny' in the BOAC Crew Room at Whitchurch while waiting to go on service. (IWM)

Dakota III G-AGHJ of BOAC, temporarily in RAF Transport Command markings with the serial number FD867, shortly after take off from Whitchurch in June 1943. (IWM)

BOAC aircrews relaxing in the Crew Room at Whitchurch, June 1943. (IWM)

up)–Gibraltar–Algiers, and routing via Rabat and Gibraltar on the return flight, this was the first of several routes flown by BOAC Dakotas in military markings with crews wearing RAF uniform. Instead of the usual civil registration letters, Dakotas operating these services carried RAF roundels and serial numbers, with white-painted Transport Command four-letter codes on their fuselage sides. Such markings were required when operating under the aegis of RAF Transport Command or when passing through places recently liberated and still under Allied military control.

Towards the end of 1943, with a massive build-up of American forces in Britain, many USAAF bomber and transport aircraft arrived via the South Atlantic route, the final leg of which was from Marrakech, Morocco, to Valley, in Anglesey. This resulted in increased German air activity over the Bay of Biscay, making even more hazardous the route between Whitchurch and Lisbon. Possibly the risk was further increased because many of the American aircraft were C-47 Skytrains, legitimate military targets that were almost identical externally to the civil DC-3s and Dakotas of KLM and BOAC. Several USAAF aircraft were intercepted including, in November, a C-47 that escaped in cloud after it was damaged by a Ju 88, but no further incidents were reported by Whitchurch-based crews.

Construction work at Whitchurch continued throughout the war

Two BOAC captains completing essential paperwork at Whitchurch. (IWM)

years. On the South Side the Bristol Aeroplane Company occupied one very large 'factory-type' building, a Bellman hangar, two small hangars and various other huts and minor buildings. Also on this side were the control tower, airport administrative offices and two passenger reception blocks. On the North Side numerous buildings and huts were erected for use as offices and workshops by BOAC, KLM and the ATA. A Type T2 hangar was shared by BOAC and KLM, and an adjacent Bellman hangar was used by the ATA. Eventually there were five hangars on this side of the airport, with one of them – the most westerly – used as a stores depot by the Bristol Aeroplane Company. This same hangar also housed the resident Tiger Moth of the Bristol University Air Squadron.

Throughout the war radio aids at Whitchurch were fairly rudimentary, at first consisting only of a D/F Station for 'homing' and descent through cloud (QGH) procedures. For more precise instrument approaches a Standard Beam Approach (SBA) transmitter was later installed near to the eastern end of the runway. Radio communications were little better and, with the exception of those operated by BOAC and KLM, few of the many other aircraft using Whitchurch were able to communicate with the control tower by 'voice' or W/T. None of the aircraft operated or ferried by the ATA were radio-equipped and, in general, take-offs and landings were controlled by visual lamp signals.

1944

During 1943 and 1944 unscheduled visitors were not uncommon at Whitchurch which, despite its obviously short runway, seemed to attract aircraft that were either lost, low on fuel, damaged, troubled by bad weather or experiencing technical problems. They included several USAAF aircraft, among them a Republic P-47 Thunderbolt fighter which landed with engine trouble. But more memorable was the arrival of an 8th Air Force B-24 Liberator which, thanks to skilful handling and clearly efficient brakes, landed safely with a full bomb load on board. The B-24 was parked on the North Side apron but because of its great weight soon began to break through the tarmac surface. Accordingly, to confine the damage, the crew opened the Liberator's bomb doors and unceremoniously dumped its un-fused bombs onto the ground. Even lightly loaded, the B-24 was considered too 'hot' to take off from a runway only 1,000 yards long, so it was later dismantled by a USAAF recovery crew and taken away on trucks. This incident followed the arrival on 23 September 1943 of two B-17F Fortresses (42-3073:LL-A and 42-29711:LG-V) of the 91st Bombardment Group. Low on fuel while returning from an attack on Nantes, they re-fuelled on the North Side, where they caused quite a stir, and then departed for their base at Bassingbourn. Unfortunately, both B-17s were later lost in attacks on Germany; 42-29711 of the 322nd Bomb Squadron was shot down during a raid on Anklam on 9 October 1943 and 42-3073 of the 401st Bomb Squadron was severely damaged and written off following an attack on Ackmar on 21 February 1944.

Refuelling a Stinson L-5 Sentinel of the USAAF. Several Sentinels were based at Whitchurch from October 1943 to June 1944 for liaison duties with the First US Army. (D Wallis)

The Piper L-4 Grasshopper, better known as the Cub, was another type of American liaison aircraft based at Whitchurch in 1944. (C W Lefever)

Two of the many RAF visitors around this time were also written off, and both were from No 3 Flying Instructor's School, Lulsgate Bottom. At 10.30 am on 15 February 1944 Oxford Mk I LW776 crashed one mile to the west of Whitchurch when both engines cut out at 300 feet shortly after take-off. In the attempted forced landing which followed it appears that the aircraft lost speed and dropped a wing as it stalled. The two occupants, F/Lt F G Garvey, DSO, DFC, and F/O L W R Rogers, were killed. About a month later, at 9.40 am on 23 March, another Oxford (HN203) of No 3 FIS came to grief at Whitchurch when it crashed into a ditch following an engine failure during a go around. Fortunately, on this occasion the two pilots on board were unhurt.

At the beginning of 1944 BOAC's 20 Dakotas were all nominally based at Whitchurch, but one was operating as a freighter out of Cairo while others flew from Leuchars where they joined, and eventually replaced, five Mosquitoes and two Hudsons operating the hazardous service over German-occupied territory to Stockholm. And it was there, while landing on 21 January, that Dakota I G-AGFZ was damaged beyond repair, but none of its passengers or crew were injured. Of the other aircraft being operated by BOAC, some of its nine Liberators were operating from Prestwick and Lyneham, but most of its other landplanes – two Lockheed 10As, two Fourteens, two Hudsons, 26 Lodestars, nine Ensigns and five Flamingos – were based overseas, as were many of its 29 flying boats. However, the UK element of BOAC was about to expand significantly, and this was to have a major effect on Whitchurch.

During the build-up to D-Day, Major C W 'Chuck' Lefever, Air Officer at US Army Group Headquarters, London, was a frequent visitor to the First US Army HQ at Clifton, sometimes flying his personally assigned L-5 Sentinel into Whitchurch from Heston. (C W Lefever)

KLM resumed its Whitchurch–Lisbon–Gibraltar service with DC-3s on 29 March 1944 and on 16 April BOAC introduced a UK–West Africa landplane service using Dakotas. The normal route was Whitchurch-St Mawgan (to uplift maximum fuel)–Lisbon–Rabat–Port Etienne–Dakar–Bathurst–Freetown-Abidjan (occasionally)–Takoradi–Accra–Lagos, but the twin-engined Dakota, with its marginal engine-out performance and a cruising speed of only 145 knots, was not the ideal aircraft for this long haul. Nor was the 23-day trip popular with crews; in addition to the heat and humidity of West Africa, much of the flight was conducted over inhospitable terrain with few emergency landing grounds and very few radio aids to navigation. Not quite so unpopular were more frequently flown trips to Cairo and Karachi, but these, too, could be demanding of both men and machines.

Compared with blacked-out wartime Bristol, where there was a shortage of most commodities, the bright lights and well stocked shops of neutral Lisbon made it a pleasant stop-over for crews. Fresh fruit, rarely seen in Britain since 1939, was readily available in the Portuguese capital and crews frequently brought some in for distribution to children in local hospitals. The fruit was usually carried in colourful raffia baskets and these appealed greatly to the female administrative staff employed at the airport; rectangular in shape, the baskets were both attractive and useful and, as such things were then virtually unobtainable in Britain, they were keenly sought by airport staff. Crew members readily responded to requests for them and before long Lisbon Baskets, as they were popularly known, were a familiar sight in the Bristol area. Much like wearing a uniform, anyone seen carrying a Lisbon Basket was instantly recognised by locals as an employee of BOAC!

The Dakotas operated by BOAC differed little from those in service with the RAF. Their well equipped, comfortable crew compartments were identical, with accommodation for a crew of four (with BOAC this comprised Captain, First Officer, Navigating Officer and Radio Officer), but unlike KLM's magnificent pre-war DC-3s, the passenger cabin of BOAC's 'Daks' left much to be desired. Fairly comfortable 1940s-style airline seats were installed in place of the side-facing bench seating of military Dakotas, but no sound-proof lining or decor of any kind was applied to the bare metal structure of the cabin interior. Nor did mixed passenger/freight loads and long-range fuel tanks installed in the forward passenger cabin of some aircraft improve matters. Cabin heating was good, but in hot climates the ventilation was inadequate, except at the rear of the cabin where draughts were usually experienced around the large double passenger/freight doors. However, in temperate latitudes and at higher altitudes the draught was less welcome.

Very much aware of the shortcomings of the Dakota's passenger cabin were the flight stewards and stewardesses then employed by BOAC. Until 1943 these had been few in number, but with expansion of the Dakota fleet the Corporation recruited a large number of young

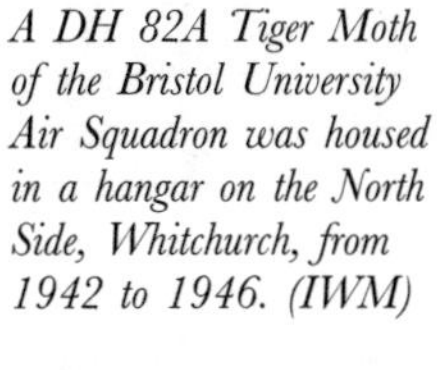

A DH 82A Tiger Moth of the Bristol University Air Squadron was housed in a hangar on the North Side, Whitchurch, from 1942 to 1946. (IWM)

Several Airspeed Oxfords, on loan from the RAF, were used by BOAC's Training School at Whitchurch for instrument flying training. (IWM)

Catering Apprentices for training as stewards. Upon reaching the age of 18 many were called-up for military service, with the result that Catering Apprentice recruitment and training were carried out at Whitchurch on an almost continuous basis.

During 1943 and 1944 many well known Hollywood film stars came to Britain to entertain American forces, with most of them arriving at Whitchurch after first flying from the USA to either Shannon or Lisbon. They included Bob Hope, Bing Crosby, Dinah Shore, Frances Langford, Joe E Brown and Edward G Robinson. Notable among the many VIPs who passed through the airport were Queen Wilhelmina of the Netherlands and Mrs Eleanor Roosevelt, wife of the US President.

On 18 April 1944 KLM celebrated its 1,000th Lisbon return service for BOAC, the flight being made by DC-3 G-AGBD *Buizerd.* The safety and regularity achieved by KLM, its fleet by now expanded to include three C-47A Dakota IIIs, owed much to its crews and ground staff, together with the inherent reliability of the DC-3, its C-47 Dakota cousin, and the Wright Cyclone and Pratt and Whitney Twin Wasp engines that respectively powered them.

In preparation for the invasion of Normandy by the Allies there was now a tremendous influx of American troops into Britain. The Headquarters of the First US Army was located at Clifton College, Bristol, and as a result American communications and transport aircraft frequently came into Whitchurch. They included Fairchild UC-61A

Forwarders and C-47 Skytrains which, although similar to the Argus and Dakota aircraft operated respectively by the ATA and BOAC, looked very different in their USAAF colours and markings. Also arriving from time to time were Cessna UC-78 Bobcat and Noorduyn UC-64A Norseman communications aircraft, but more frequently seen were Piper L-4 Cubs and Stinson L-5 Sentinels belonging, in the main, to the 153rd Liaison Squadron. This was a US 9th Air Force unit attached to the First Army for general liaison duties including daily priority mail runs and the transportation of couriers and key personnel. Several of the 153rd's aircraft were based at Whitchurch where, until they departed for Normandy in June, they shared the South Side hangar used by the BAC as its Flight Shed. By D-Day HQ First Army and its 153rd Liaison Squadron had departed, to be replaced almost immediately by HQ Ninth US Army and the 125th Liaison Squadron, but by the end of August these too had left for France.

Looking back to the pre D-Day period, former Major Thomas K Turner, then a liaison pilot with the US Army's 58th Field Artillery Battalion, remembers an amusing encounter that took place while flying his L-4 Cub (43-29618) from an airstrip at Charborough Park, near Poole, to Whitchurch. He was visiting a friend stationed in Bristol and recalls: "About 15 miles south of Whitchurch I saw an RAF Taylorcraft Auster a short distance away to my right. As we neared the airfield we converged until the Auster pilot and I could wave and make hand signals to one another. Upon arrival we landed in tandem, the Auster first, and I followed it to the parking area. There, to my pleasant surprise,

Interested ATA pilots and ground staff gather around a Boeing B-17F Fortress at Whitchurch, while a second B-17 taxies in. Based at Bassingbourn and belonging to the 91st Bomb Group, they arrived on 23 September 1943, low on fuel while returning from a raid on Nantes. (M Olmsted via A Hartles)

B-17F Fortress 42-3073 (LL-A) at Whitchurch, with Dundry Hill in the background. Piloted by 1/Lt. Gibbons, this was one of the two 91st Bomb Group Fortresses that arrived unexpectedly on 23 September 1943. (M Olmsted via A Hartles)

the Auster pilot turned out to be a cute little blonde female ferry pilot! As we strolled to Ops together we talked and I fell madly in love. But now, 50 years later, I don't even remember her name – and she probably doesn't remember mine either!"

Another recollection of the 1944 period comes from former BOAC fitter Bernard Morey, who wrote: "From time to time Dakotas *(sic)* of the American Air Force would drop in, after the invasion of Europe had begun, to acquire booze for their personnel in France. The Dakota would land, the doors would open and ramps carried internally in the aircraft would be placed in position. Then a Jeep would drive out, and away went the crew to their destination. If we had been asked to put those ramps into position we would have needed crow bars, shoring and goodness knows what – and most likely it would have taken us all day!". Recalling the condition of the aircraft, Bernard Morey continued: "The insides of those Dakotas' engine cowlings had to be seen to be believed. The cylinders were thick with red earth and sand and it was obvious the cowlings had not been removed for days. When the crew returned from their mission to the pub it was a matter of drive in the Jeep, up with the ramps, shut the doors, and away. No fuss at all – and they didn't even do a full engine run-up before take-off!". All of which was seemingly typical of the Americans, their apparently casual attitude disguising an expertise which in practice probably matched that of BOAC with its immaculate aeroplanes and strict adherence to laid down procedures.

Accidents were few at Whitchurch, but a serious one on 10 July 1944 again involved an RAF aircraft from No 3 FIS, Lulsgate Bottom. On this occasion it was a Miles Master II (W9067) that collided with a US Army L-5 Sentinel as both aircraft were approaching to land. The L-5 was ahead of the Master, but apparently neither pilot saw the other and after colliding both aircraft crashed on the airfield and burnt out, injuring the two occupants in each.

How this accident occurred is something of a mystery as take-offs and landings at Whitchurch were normally controlled by visual Aldis lamp signals from a runway controller at the Airfield Control Point (ACP). In this instance the L-5 should have received a steady green signal, clearing it to land, and the Master a steady red, warning its pilot to go around. Failure to comply with a red lamp signal was normally followed by a red flare, fired from a Very pistol, but on this occasion the system appears not to have worked.

At Whitchurch, as at wartime RAF airfields, the ACP was a black and white chequered van, modified to incorporate an observation position. Parked alongside the active runway near the touchdown point, the ACP was connected by telephone landline to the control tower, where the duty flying control officer exercised overall supervision. Perhaps surprisingly, in view of the responsible nature of their work, the runway controllers at Whitchurch in 1944-45 were young Air Training Corps cadets who, in addition to their runway control function, also assisted pilots to land in misty or foggy conditions by firing white pyrotechnics into the air and along the runway. With no approach or runway lighting to assist them, visual guidance of this nature, initiated when the aircraft's engines were heard on final approach, was of great value to pilots landing in poor visibility. Like the flying control officers of that period, the ATC Cadet runway controllers at Whitchurch were employed by the Air Ministry.

On 27 June BOAC's UK–Algiers Dakota service was extended to Cairo (operating Whitchurch–St Mawgan–Gibraltar–Algiers–Tripoli-Cairo), but Algiers was omitted as a stop on the route from 1 October. However, aviation continued to take its toll and on 28 August Whitchurch-based Dakota III G-AGIR was lost while operating a West African service. It crashed at Telmest, in the foothills of the Atlas Mountains near Casablanca, killing Capt L J M White, Second Officer L Thompson, Navigating Officer G F Taylor, Radio Officer L A Graham and three passengers.

At Whitchurch itself accidents were mercifully few, but an incident on 17 September might well have had unfortunate consequences for passengers in a bus travelling along the Wells Road. In bad weather, and just as it was getting dark, Boulton Paul Defiant R3421 arrived at Whitchurch from Desford, flown by Capt Bill Cuthbert of the ATA. The rear seat of the Defiant – a target towing conversion of the one-time night fighter – was occupied by Flight Engineer Paul Longthorp, who later recalled: "The view ahead was non existent and in my efforts to see forward as we approached the runway, I was horrified to see my foot dislodge the crash axe, which disappeared through the hole in the floor through which target drogues were released. My horror increased as I noticed a grey double-decker bus passing underneath and imagined the carnage which might result. Subsequently no one would even listen to my story, saying 'We'll know soon enough when the police return the axe'. It never showed up again, but I was more careful after that".

On 7 October KLM personnel at Whitchurch celebrated the 25th anniversary of their airline's foundation. The company was able to look back on 25 years of great success in the air transport business, but none of those years had been more valuable or more demanding than the past four spent in exile. Since July 1940 the small but highly efficient KLM fleet had completed 2,250 flights on the hazardous Lisbon route, with no fuss or publicity but justifiably earning awards of the OBE or MBE for five members of its staff.

Meanwhile, on the Continent great developments were taking place. Much of Western France was liberated that autumn and on 9 October flights in daylight were resumed to and from Lisbon. Further, the long 10° West crossing of the Bay of Biscay was no longer necessary and on 25 October a KLM Dakota, operating the most direct route between Whitchurch and Lisbon, set a new record with a flight time of 4 hrs 4 mins. This followed the first direct non-stop service from Whitchurch to Madrid on 23 October, operated by a Dakota commanded by Capt N

Staff of BOAC's Navigation Branch in their wartime accommodation in Trafalgar House, Clifton, Bristol. Maps and Route Manuals for all BOAC flights were prepared and issued by this office. (Mrs J Vogler)

Steen. Henceforward, similar direct flights were to be carried out twice weekly.

The departure of the Germans from Norway and Denmark also permitted Dakotas to take over all the Leuchars–Stockholm services previously flown by Whitleys, Hudsons and Mosquitoes. Flights to other European cities also began, one of the first being to Paris (Le Bourget) by Whitchurch-based Dakotas operating through Croydon.

The BOAC Central Training School on the North Side of Whitchurch had been extremely busy for some time, among other things training seconded RAF aircrew personnel. Type conversion and other flight training was carried out from the South Side, using Dakotas temporarily taken off line service and four Airspeed Oxfords on loan from the RAF. By October 1943 these had been replaced by five more Oxford IIs, but by November 1944 the CTS fleet comprised six Oxfords and two semi-permanent Dakotas (G-AGKC and G-AGKE). Many of the seconded RAF crews had extensive operational experience with Bomber and Coastal Commands but Whitchurch, with its single runway of only 1,000 yards, was far from ideal for Dakota conversions. However, pilots trained on such a runway were unlikely to experience landing difficulties elsewhere on the route system.

Sunday, 17 September 1944, saw the arrival at Whitchurch of Lodestar OO-CAV from the Belgian Congo, marking the opening of a new monthly service by the Belgian airline Sabena. Under the command of the company's Chief Pilot, Capt J Van Aaker, the 18-seat aircraft had departed Leopoldville, the home of the exiled Belgian airline since 1940, and flew via Lagos, Kano, Aoulef, Casablanca and Lisbon. The Lodestar left on its return flight on 24 September and a second service arrived on 10 October. By May 1945 nine round trips had been completed, but shortly afterwards the European terminus of the route was changed to liberated Brussels.

Another unfamiliar uniform seen at Whitchurch around this time indicated the arrival of some TAP Portuguese Airlines pilots for Dakota conversion training, but RAF uniforms predominated in November 1944 when secondments to BOAC were further increased. This coincided with the arrival of some new C-47B Dakota Mk IVs (the first of 23 aircraft registered G-AGKA to G-AGKN, G-AGMZ, G-AGNA to G-AGNG, and G-AGNK). Apart from lengthened engine air intakes, the Mk IVs differed little externally from earlier versions, but Twin Wasp R-1830-9OC engines with two-speed superchargers improved their performance at high altitude. Internally they were also basically similar to the Mk III, with few noticeable changes. By 1944 standards both versions were very well equipped, their comprehensive radio installations including a radio compass and the three receivers (localiser, glide-path and marker beacon) of the SCS 51 instrument landing system (later known as ILS). A radio altimeter was also installed, together with communications equipment comprising a long range Liaison set and two shorter range (VHF and MF) Command sets. Essential equipment in the navigator's position included a repeater compass, a centrally

AIR TRANSPORT AUXILIARY
No. 2 FERRY POOL, March, 1944

Back Row, L. to R.—Ft/Eng. P. Longthorp. S/O Ashburner. L. S/O F. Symondson. F/O T. Blake. F/O R. Ayres. S/O C. Whicher. S/O P. Frisby. S/O E. West. T/O P. Robertson Rodger. S/O C. Nichols. S/O N. Fryer. S/O N. Sisley. S/O J. Ball. F/O P. Nowlan. T/O J. Innes.

Middle Row, L. to R.—F/O L. Biggs. F/O C. Hay. F/O R. Roberts. Ft/Eng. J. Clarey. F/O B. Robins. F/O P. Cruttenden. F/O A. Green. F/O W. Riley. F/O M. Armstrong. F/O D. Coopper. S/O B. Harrison. F/O K. Jones. F/O J. Wood. F/O W. Warrington. Ft/Eng. C. Parker. Ft/Eng. A. K. Clarke. Ft/Eng. G. Verrall. S/O E. Iredale. F/O R. Hosking. F/O M. Hill. F/O S. Roy. F/O E. Shine.

Front Row, L. to R.—S/O G. Wigley. T/O T. Rolling. F/O D. Richardson, F/O P. Grenside. F/O W. Turle. Ft/Capt. W. Cuthbert. S/O H. Penchoen. F/O S. Mill. Ft/Capt. A. Unwin. Capt. G. Pine. Commander L. Leaver. Ft/Capt. J. Hope. Ft/Capt. G. Dutton. Ft/Capt. E. Mogridge. F/O L. Burch. F/O J. Drzewiecki. F/O A. Rogers. F/O L. Kemp. F/O A. Ward. F/O H. Rowe. T/O H. Dutton.

OPPOSITE *Whitchurch-based ATA pilots and flight engineers of No. 2 Ferry Pool, March 1944. (L Burch via A J Pitchers)*

located astrodome, and an APN-2 *Rebecca* radar interrogating set. *Rebecca*, a short range navigation and aerodrome approach aid, remained a closely guarded secret until the end of the war, with the result that wartime photographs of Dakotas were 'doctored' by the Censor to remove any sign of the H-type *Rebecca* antennae mounted below the pilots' windows on both sides of the fuselage.

The delivery of 23 Mk IVs eventually brought the number of Dakotas based at Whitchurch to 57. In practice some of this fleet, now designated No 1 Line with Mr E P Hessey as Line Manager, operated from other stations with, by March 1945, five at Cairo, ten at Croydon and five at Leuchars. Their absence meant no lessening of work for the Engineering Branch, however, as other types, including Hudsons and Lodestars from Leuchars and Cairo, came to Whitchurch for major maintenance and Certificate of Airworthiness renewals.

From a total of 109 aircraft (landplanes and flying boats) on 1 January 1943, BOAC's fleet had increased to 140 by the end of 1944, with about 40 per cent of then nominally based at Whitchurch. However, the writing was on the wall when Hurn, near Bournemouth, was named as BOAC's future main UK operations base. Unlike Whitchurch, Hurn's runways were long enough to accommodate the Corporation's Liberators and the new Avro Yorks and Lancastrians then coming into service. Nevertheless, although Hurn became the passenger departure point from November 1944, Whitchurch was to remain the home station and maintenance base of BOAC's Dakota fleet for some years to come.

On 5 December the Corporation operated its first Hurn–Gibraltar service in place of KLM, who ceased their Whitchurch operations on 31 December. The comparatively little used DC-2 G-AGBH then received the military serial NL293 and departed for service with the Netherlands Government. KLM's three Dakotas and two of its original DC-3s also returned to Holland, although both DC-3s returned to the UK in 1946 under the ownership of Skyways, Ltd.

As the war entered its final stages Whitchurch experienced what was probably its most spectacular accident. This involved an RAF Halifax B Mk III which became lost in the thick haze of a quiet Saturday afternoon when most of the airport staff were taking a welcome weekend break. In sunny but very hazy conditions the Halifax made two unsuccessful attempts to land in an easterly direction, but came in too high each time because of the poor visibility and a very light wind. On a third attempt it was again too high, but continued its approach and touched down nearly half-way along the runway. As the bomber approached the eastern perimeter track, with little runway remaining and still going very fast, it swung to the left, continued across the grass and then struck a sunken concrete pillbox situated between the runway and the North Side apron. On impact one undercarriage leg collapsed and as it swung around the Halifax began to disintegrate, the fuselage breaking into three sections and the right wing rising to a near vertical position before crashing back down in a cloud of flying earth and dust.

A C-47B Skytrain and crew of the 440th Troop Carrier Group, US 9th Air Force. Following the Normandy landings Skytrains occasionally landed at Whitchurch, usually on legitimate business but sometimes on unofficial 'booze runs'! (J Bos)

Hardly had the wreckage come to a standstill when, to the astonishment of the few airport staff who witnessed the crash, the seven-man crew emerged from the shattered fuselage. Helping one of their number who was slightly hurt, they hurried away from the immediate vicinity of the aircraft but luckily there was no fire and the bombs allegedly on board did not explode.

It is surprising that there were not more accidents at Whitchurch, where the short runway was not compatible with some of the heavy bombers and high performance fighters flown in by pilots of No 2 Ferry Pool. This says much for the mixed band of civilian pilots of the ATA who, with only Handling Notes to guide them went from type to type with no proper individual aircraft conversion training. Further, they often flew several different types in one day and these could vary enormously in size and performance. Pilots were graded, with the lesser experienced initially restricted to simple single-engine aircraft, but as they gained experience instructional courses on representative twin- and, eventually, four-engine aircraft broadly prepared them to fly the various types of aircraft in each category. Despite the limitations of this training, ATA pilots coped extremely well, but bad weather and engine and other technical failures took a heavy toll during the five years of the ATA's existence.

A typical Whitchurch-based ATA pilot was First Officer A W 'Bert' Harris of Wembworthy, Devon. Bert Harris obtained his 'A' Licence in

1935, but because of slightly defective vision was not accepted for flying duties with the RAF when the war started. Instead he became a Link Trainer Instructor, but following the fall of France there was an urgent need for pilots and he was then accepted for non-operational flying duties. In June 1941 Harris was transferred to the ATA and after training on Magisters, Tiger Moths and Oxfords served with Ferry Pools at Ratcliffe and Sherburn. He was posted to No 2 Ferry Pool at Whitchurch on 24 October 1942, on which day, his personal flying log book reveals, he positioned to Chivenor to fly Tiger Moth DE453 to Whitchurch. From here he flew Oxford L9695 to Cardiff and then returned to Whitchurch with Hurricane HW469. The following day, the 25th, was typical of those to come; after positioning to Wroughton he delivered a Spitfire to Prestwick and the following day returned to Whitchurch with Wellington Z8823. Bert Harris often acted as a 'taxi' pilot, flying Anson and Fairchild Argus aircraft, but on ferry trips he flew many different types in and out of Whitchurch, among them Blenheims, Battles, Whitleys, Masters, Hurricanes, Spitfires, Lysanders, Tiger Moths, Magisters, Austers, Proctors, Beaufighters, Wellingtons and Oxfords. Less commonly seen types that he ferried through Whitchurch were Stinson Reliants, Avro Tutors, a Hart, a Beaufort and an Albemarle.

Periods of bad weather and the short daylight hours of winter frequently produced backlogs of aircraft awaiting delivery and the pilots of No 2 Ferry Pool then worked especially hard to clear them. Leave and even days off were cancelled when the occasion demanded, and despite their civilian status public holidays meant little. For example, on Christmas Eve 1942 Bert Harris made two trips with Spitfires from Yeovilton to Brize Norton, on Christmas Day he flew Whitley LA814 from St Athan to Whitchurch, and on Christmas Eve 1943 ferried two Beaufighters (NE431 and NE429) from Weston to Whitchurch. During his time with the ATA he flew 1,209 hours on 67 different types of aircraft and completed 660 deliveries, not all of which were without incident. Typically, on 19 December 1943 a systems failure in Seafire LN815 resulted in Bert Harris landing at Whitchurch without flaps and brakes, and on 21 January 1944, while flying Wellington HZ117 from Dumfries to Kemble, he was struck by lightning.

From May 1945, with the end of the war in Europe, there was a decline in ATA activity at Whitchurch and No 2 Ferry Pool ceased operations altogether in September. By then the organisation as a whole had ferried 308,567 aircraft of 147 different types, sadly losing 154 pilots and flight engineers of both sexes in the process.

CHAPTER SEVEN

The Post-War Years

1945–1957

The war in Europe came to an end in May 1945 but in many ways BOAC continued to operate on a war footing. Some things did change, however, including the paint scheme of its aircraft; a new style Speedbird insignia – with two horizontal white bars and the lettering 'BOAC' – was introduced and the sombre camouflage was replaced by an overall silver finish with black lettering.

The Air Ministry relinquished control of Whitchurch in June, the Director General of Civil Aviation then assuming responsibility for its operation, with Air Traffic Control and other technical services ultimately coming under a newly established Ministry of Civil Aviation.

In September 1945 the BOAC Dakota fleet was joined by three Halifax C Mk VIII freighters, which arrived in RAF markings with the serial numbers PP325, PP326 and PP327, but Whitchurch was clearly too small for these four-engined aircraft, even when lightly loaded. Accordingly, arrangements were made for them to operate from Weston Airport, where a temporary maintenance base was established, with personnel on detachment from Whitchurch and hangarage provided by the Bristol Aeroplane Company. The Halifaxes then began freight services to Accra, via Hurn, at which airport they were based from November 1945.

The general restriction on civil flying was lifted on 1 January 1946, by which time the end was in sight for flying training by BOAC at Whitchurch. A ground school remained on the North Side, providing technical courses for pilots and engineers, but flying training was to be transferred to Aldermaston, Berkshire, where a Central Training School (later to become Airways Training, Ltd.) was established. The Oxfords and training Dakotas duly departed and with the formation of BOAC's European Division, which later became British European Airways (BEA), more Dakotas left Whitchurch, bound for Northolt. Phase 1 of this move was initiated on 4 February with the transfer of 52 staff and 13 Dakotas. A further five Dakotas left for Northolt when Phase 2 was implemented on 25 February, followed by Phase 3 and the departure of one more aircraft on 11 March.

With the end of the war the private road between the Airport Road and Whitchurch Lane had been re-opened to the public. This greatly

Some of the office, technical and operations staff of BOAC's No. 1 Line, Whitchurch, in 1947. (BOAC)

facilitated access to the airport's South Side, where the wartime passenger terminal remained in use. Unlike immediate pre-war days, however, early post-war domestic air services from Whitchurch were feeble in the extreme, consisting only of scheduled flights to Cardiff and Southampton by Rapides of Great Western and Southern Airlines. Services commenced in July 1946 but the following year, following the nationalisation of Great Western and Southern Airlines and its absorption into BEA, both routes were declared uneconomical and operations ceased.

With the long awaited resumption of private flying, the Bristol and Wessex Aeroplane Club re-occupied its pre-war Club House and commenced operations in the autumn with the first of three ex-RAF Taylorcraft Auster Is, known in civilian guise as Taylorcraft Plus Model Ds. The CFI was F/Lt J H Wingate Hill, AFC, who had gained his 'B' Licence with the Club in 1936, and the Secretary was the late Leonard R Williams. 'Willie' as he was widely known, had also been connected with both the airport and the Club since the 1930s and with the departure of Capt L P Winters in 1943 was appointed Airport Manager. A popular figure, he was to hold the post until the airport closed, whereupon he became the first Manager of Bristol's new airport at Lulsgate Bottom.

Despite the severe austerity of the early post war period, with petrol rationing and other wartime restrictions still in force, the Club managed to survive and over the next three years added two Auster J/1 Autocrats and a Tiger Moth to its fleet. On 17 May 1947 the Club re-introduced

OPPOSITE *Engineers of No. 1 Line, Whitchurch, with Dakotas recently repainted in BOAC's first post-war silver finish. In 1946 the nearest aircraft, G-AGHM, went to the European Division of BOAC, which duly became BEA. In 1959 it returned to operate services from Bristol with Cambrian Airways, a BEA subsidiary company. (B J Morey)*

its traditional Garden Party and, as in pre-war days, this involved No 501 Squadron, now back at Filton with Spitfire LF XVIs as part of the Royal (as it now was) Auxiliary Air Force.

The Bristol Aeroplane Company still occupied one hangar on the North Side and much of the South Side, where it planned to extend its engine overhaul facility, but so far as airline operations were concerned the outlook for the airport was bleak. A return to London by all departments of BOAC also seemed imminent, and not only from Whitchurch. From the earliest days of the war there had been a substantial BOAC presence in Bristol itself, where the Grand Spa Hotel (now the Avon Gorge Hotel) at Clifton served as the Corporation's Headquarters. Several very large houses in the area had also been acquired for offices, with one of them – Trafalgar House, located in particularly attractive surroundings in The Promenade – occupied by the Operations Department's Navigation Branch under Capt E Brook Williams. Among other things it was here that intelligence material was gathered from Air Ministry and other sources to update the maps and route/aerodrome information manuals that were issued to the crews of every landplane and flying boat service departing the United Kingdom. Later on that same Department was 'semi-divorced' from BOAC to become the Aerad company of today, supplying aeronautical information and documentation to civil aviation on a world-wide basis as part of British Airways.

Although BOAC had initiated the return of some staff to London in mid-1944, Bristol remained an active station with 14 Dakota services – including the long hauls to Cairo and West Africa – originating from

Whitchurch-based Dakota III G-AGHE carries the revised Speedbird insignia that accompanied BOAC's first post-war colour scheme. (BOAC)

Whitchurch in the early 1950s. With the exception of the Control Tower, Admin. Offices, Club House and passenger buildings (all painted white), much of the South Side was occupied by the Bristol Aeroplane Company during the war. On the North (far) Side, the hangar on the left was also used by the BAC; beside it is the former ATA hangar and the white painted ATA Operations Block, later used by BOAC's Stores Section and the Airways Aero Club. The hangar to the right of this was shared by KLM and BOAC, with the latter occupying the remaining North Side hangars and buildings. (Author's Collection)

Whitchurch until August 1946. Thereafter Whitchurch continued as a maintenance base, its Dakotas positioning to and from Hurn, Croydon and Aldermaston, as required, but Hurn was soon to be replaced by London (Heathrow) for all international arrivals and departures. And it was on a positioning flight from London's new airport to Whitchurch on 3 January 1947 that Dakota III G-AGJV was badly damaged. After landing it swung off the runway onto wet grass and then skidded over undulating ground, causing its landing gear to collapse. None of the crew or staff passengers on board were injured, but the aircraft was a write-off.

After eight years of occupation BOAC aircraft finally left Whitchurch, but the Corporation's association with the airport was not at an end because the Technical Training School and a large Stores Depot were to remain for some time to come. Further, at the beginning of 1949 BOAC's presence in the Bristol area was re-established in strength when No 3 Line arrived at Filton from Montreal, its Lockheed 049 and 749 Constellations being joined later in the year by Boeing B.377 Stratocruisers.

Filton was to be the maintenance base for the Constellation/Stratocruiser Fleet for the next four years and to provide flying club facilities for staff employed at both Filton and the Stores Depot at Whitchurch, a Bristol Branch of the Airways Aero Club was formed. Hangarage and other accommodation was provided by the Stores Depot at Whitchurch, with a club room and office in the building formerly occupied by the now disbanded ATA. Operations commenced in April 1949 with Miles Hawk Trainer III G-AKKZ, one of five war surplus Magisters (the RAF name for the Hawk Trainer) purchased in 1948 by Airways Aero Associations, Ltd., the BOAC Associate Company formed to operate the Airways Aero Club.

From this modest single aircraft beginning, the Bristol Branch of the Club (there were also Branches at Denham and Hurn) went on to operate a unique collection of aeroplanes, some of which were privately owned but made available to Club members. Initially, Stratocruiser pilot Capt Geoff Liles acted as CFI, assisted by First Officer Bill Kemp and Engineer Officer H 'Mac' MacDonnell, but towards the end of 1949 Rex J Downes was appointed CFI, with Vernon Horseman as Chief Engineer. The Club eventually operated three Hawk Trainer IIIs,

In 1947, following the absorption of Great Western and Southern Airlines into the newly formed British European Airways, this Bedford coach (painted in BEA colours) was used to carry passengers between the Centre, Temple Meads Station and Whitchurch. (M J Tozer Collection)

Taylorcraft Plus Model D G-AHWK, acquired by the Bristol and Wessex Aeroplane Club in 1946. (A J Pitchers)

Miles M.14A Hawk Trainer III G-AFBS of the Airways Aero Club, Whitchurch, 1950. (W K Kilsby)

The red and silver Aeronca 100 G-AEXD of the Airways Aero Club, parked in front of the wartime ATA parachute store at Whitchurch. (W K Kilsby)

an Aeronca 100, a Puss Moth, an Auster V, a Piper J3 Cub, a Percival Proctor 3 and, for a short period, a Tiger Moth on loan from the Hurn Branch. Subsidised by BOAC, flying charges were about half the rate charged by other clubs, with further reductions for members who voluntarily worked on the aircraft or otherwise assisted in running the club.

As in pre-war days, regular air displays were organised at Whitchurch by the Bristol and Wessex Club, with that held on 25 September 1948 featuring a Sprint Race for Auster aircraft. However, on 23 September 1950 the Airways Aero Club joined forces with the Bristol and Wessex Club for a combined Garden Party and Flying Display. The programme opened with an exhibition of 'crazy flying' by Joe Wingate Hill of the Wessex Club, followed by a demonstration of SkyJeep G-AKVS by Mr D Lowry of the Chrislea Aircraft Co Ltd. As usual, No 501 Squadron took part, but in place of Spitfires the squadron was now flying Vampire jet fighters. Equally impressive, but in a very different way, were low fly-pasts by a Constellation and a Stratocruiser, proof positive of the Airways Aero Club's involvement in the afternoon's entertainment.

Another interesting arrival that day was the Airways Aero Club's eight-seat Dragon I, G-ACIT, flown by Capt John Lobley, the founder of the Club, and carrying several Denham Branch members. The Dragon, a rarity in 1950 but at one time the most commonly seen airliner at Whitchurch, was available to Club members with more than 150 hours flying experience for the astonishingly low charge of £3.15s.0d (£3.75p) an hour. Fortunately this superb old aircraft, which first went into service with Highland Airways in 1934, survived the rigours of club flying and is now part of the Science Museum's collection of historic transport aircraft at Wroughton.

Two of the former Whitchurch-based Hawk Trainer IIIs have also

Puss Moth G-AEOA, with the winged emblem of the Airways Aero Club on its engine cowling. (W K Kilsby)

Taylorcraft Auster V G-AJVU, owned by John Shuckburgh but on loan to the Bristol Branch of the Airways Aero Club. The former ATA hangar and Operations Block can be seen in the background. (W K Kilsby)

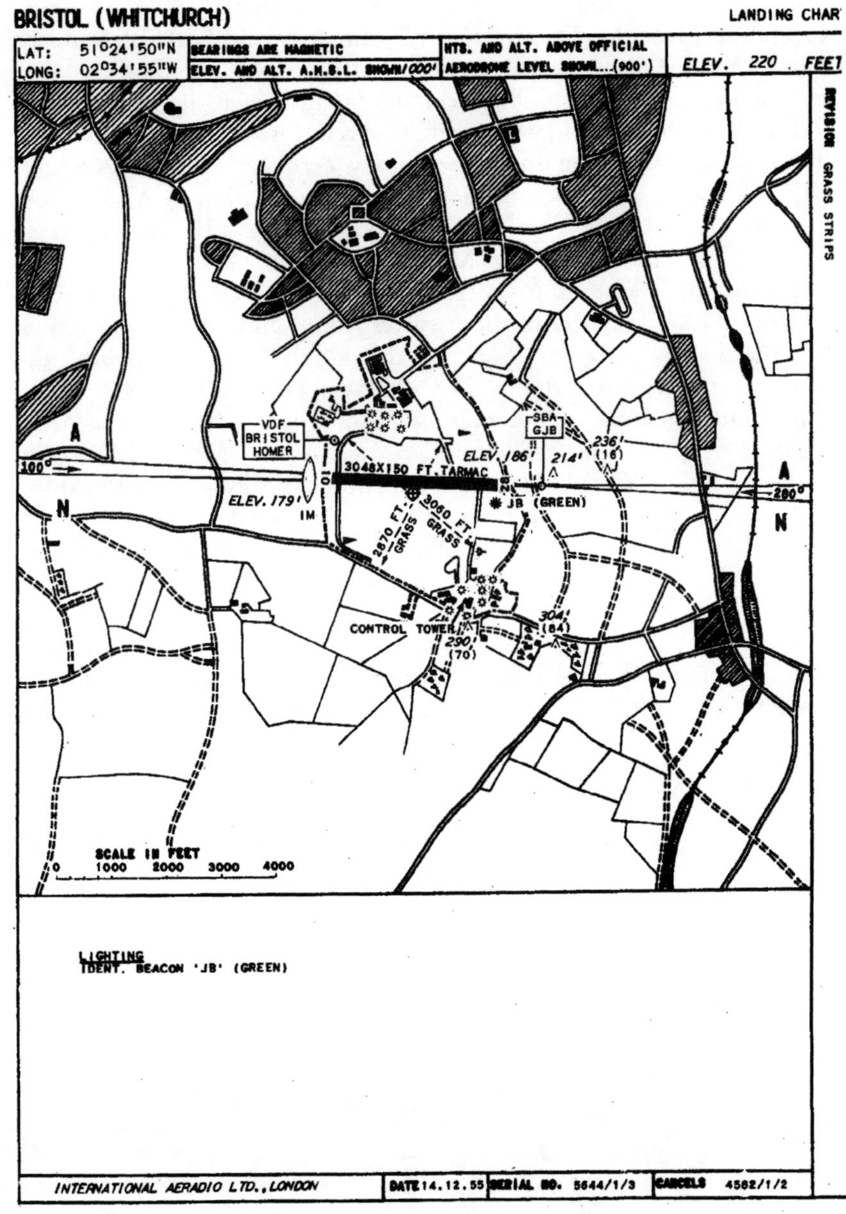

The 1955 Landing Chart for Whitchurch Airport. (Author's Collection)

survived to become museum exhibits, G-AKKR being with the Greater Manchester Museum of Science and Technology and G-AFBS with the Imperial War Museum at Duxford. As both are ex-RAF Magisters they are now in wartime camouflage colours (as they were upon arrival by road at Whitchurch in 1949), with G-AKKR restored as T9967. In 1950, during its overhaul and airworthiness certification, the second aircraft (RAF serial BB661) was allocated the registration G-AKKU, but it was then found to be a pre-war civil Hawk Trainer III that had been impressed into the RAF as a Magister in 1939. Accordingly, it was re-allocated the registration G-AFBS, originally issued to it in 1937.

Aeronca 100 G-AEXD of the Airways Aero Club is another survivor from those early post-war days at Whitchurch, as is the Bristol and Wessex Club's Taylorcraft Plus D G-AHWJ. The former is still flying, in private ownership, while the latter is now with the Museum of Army Flying at Middle Wallop, restored as an Auster Mk I (LB294) in wartime RAF markings. Another Whitchurch survivor is Avro Anson Mk I N4877, formerly with the ATA's No 2 Ferry Pool and now owned by the Imperial War Museum. Nor does the surprising number of Whitchurch-associated survivors stop there, for Puss Moth G-AEOA still flies from Old Warden, despite being 'grounded' by the Airways Aero Club at Whitchurch in 1950. This followed a report that one wing was seen to move slightly upwards while in flight near Bristol. Following a gentle but expeditious return to Whitchurch, inspection revealed

Passengers from Jersey disembarking at Whitchurch in 1954. The aircraft is Rapide G-AKUB Glamorgan *of Cambrian Air Services. (D Loader)*

The Cambrian Rapide G-ALZJ Caernarvon, *on the South Side apron at Whitchurch in 1955. (A J Pitchers)*

Dakota IV G-AMSX of CAS at Whitchurch, 1955. (A J Pitchers)

Little changed from wartime – a 1955 view of the South Side apron with the control tower and BAC engine overhaul building in the background. The Customs Hall and passenger recption buildings are in front of the tower. (Author)

A Tiger Moth of the Bristol and Wessex Aeroplane Club, beside the Clubhouse in 1955. (Author)

partial failure of a wing attachment bracket. According to the local Air Registration Board Surveyor then responsible for airworthiness certification of the Club's aircraft, there was no approved repair scheme for this failure and as a result the aircraft was grounded. As a source for spare parts it was then sold to a company at Blackpool for the princely sum of £45 and duly departed Whitchurch by road. Shortly afterwards, however, word reached the Club that the Puss Moth was flying again, on a Public Transport Certificate of Airworthiness and carrying out joy-rides around Blackpool Tower! Clearly, ARB Surveyors in different parts of the country were not always of the same mind with regard to repair schemes.

The pre-war creation of housing estates by Bristol Corporation had seen a steady encroachment on land surrounding the airport and this was further exacerbated in post-war years. This, and the proximity of Dundry Hill, ruled out any possibility of extending the airport to accommodate modern heavy aircraft, so Filton and Lulsgate Bottom (used only by the Bristol Gliding Club since the departure of the RAF) now came under review as possible replacements for Whitchurch.

In 1950 the re-formed Airport Committee, concerned at the absence of air services from Bristol, made strenuous efforts to remedy the situation. At that time scheduled flights were entirely the prerogative of the two national airlines, BEA and BOAC, with private companies restricted to charter operations only. However, as a result of the pressure applied by the Airport Committee, the Ministry of Civil Aviation granted a licence to Morton Air Services, Ltd., of Croydon to operate associate scheduled services from Whitchurch to the Channel

A 1955 view of the Club hangar and Club House. (Author)

Islands, the Isle of Man and the Isle of Wight. Using mainly Airspeed Consuls, the company carried 2,500 passengers that year, when charters were also undertaken to various European destinations.

As part of Bristol's 1951 Festival of Britain celebrations the Bristol and Wessex and Airways Aero Clubs again joined forces for an air display on 14 July. The Vampires of No 501 Squadron gave a most impressive display, as did S/Ldr W 'Dusty' Miller, the CFI of No 12 Reserve Flying School, Filton, in a superb exhibition of 'crazy' flying in a Tiger Moth. Of particular interest was a 1917 Bristol 'Fighter' flown by A J 'Bill' Pegg, the Chief Test Pilot of the Bristol Aeroplane Company, while at the other end of the size range the US Third Air Force provided a fly-past by a Boeing B-50 Superfortress. There were numerous other events including a Bristol Air Race and demonstrations by Royal Navy Seafires of No 1832 (RNVR) Squadron from Culham and Sea Furies and Fireflies of No 767 Squadron, Yeovilton.

Despite its primary function of providing flying facilities for employees of BOAC, much of the Airways Aero Club's activity at Whitchurch was in connection with an 'in house' scheme to train redundant BOAC navigators as pilots. As a first step, participating Navigating Officers were required to obtain a Private Pilot's Licence and use was made of the Club's Hawk Trainers for this purpose. However, Airways Aero Club activity at Whitchurch came to an end when the Stratocruiser/Constellation Fleet left Filton for Heathrow.

The Bristol and Wessex Aeroplane Club, now with Harry Armitage as CFI, continued to prosper and in 1953 Tiger Moth G-AMBK was replaced by G-AJHU, another aircraft of the same type. This was

Dove G-AJOT of Cambrian Airways at Whitchurch in 1956. The large building beyond the control tower was occupied by the Bristol Aeroplance Company wing and for some years after the war. (A J Pitchers)

An aeroplane 'spotter's' view of the South Side tarmac, seen from Whitchurch Lane, with a Cambrian Dove about to depart. (A J Pitchers)

The Shell/BP aviation fuel station on the South Side, Whitchurch, in 1957. (A J Pitchers)

The DH 114 Heron was one of the few four-engined aircraft to use Whitchurch. This new Mk 2, G-AOGO, entered service with Cambrian in 1956.
(Cambrian Airways)

joined by another Tiger Moth, G-ANSM, in 1955. Clearly, despite the comfort and other advantages of cabin aircraft like the Autocrat, there was still a demand for open cockpit biplanes, a situation which prevails to this day.

There was still no indication that BEA would return to operate services from Whitchurch, but on 3 May 1951 Aer Lingus commenced a DC-3 service to Dublin. That same year Morton Air Services received approval to operate services from Bristol to Paris via Southampton, and this route continued to be flown in 1952, with additional services to the Channel Islands. Similar associate scheduled services were being flown from Croydon by Olley Air Service and in 1953 this company merged with Morton Air Services. Rationalisation of routes and aircraft followed, and this resulted in Cambrian Air Services (CAS) of Cardiff acquiring Morton's Bristol operation and taking over its services to Paris and the Channel Islands. CAS had long wanted to operate from Bristol and with its acquisition of these routes the company purchased two DH 104 Doves and two Rapides from Olley Air Service. In addition two Consuls were acquired from Morton Air Services, but they were sold shortly afterwards and did not go into service with the Welsh airline.

Formed by Mr S Kenneth Davies in 1935, Cambrian Air Services, Ltd., had tried to join Western Airways on the Cardiff-Weston service before the war, but because of opposition from WA failed to do so until 1948. Ansons of Western Airways then flew in parallel with the Rapides of CAS, but two years later, when WA virtually ceased flying operations to become a maintenance facility, CAS assumed sole responsibility for the service. The end came, however, with the acquisition of new routes by Cambrian and the decision to close conveniently located Pengam Moors airport at Cardiff in favour of a new Cardiff Airport located some 12 miles distant at Rhoose, near Barry.

Between 1953 and 1957 a rapidly expanding CAS built-up an extensive route network from Cardiff and Bristol, its seven Rapides eventually being replaced by three Doves, a DH 114 Heron I, three Heron IIs and two Dakotas. Much of the airline's success was due to its founder, S Kenneth Davies, an enthusiastic private pilot and one-time Chairman of the Royal Aero Club. He was also Chairman of the Welsh Advisory Council for Civil Aviation and in 1951 was appointed to the Board of BEA. This required 'SKD' as the popular Welshman was widely known, to resign his position as Managing Director of CAS, but by no means did he lose interest in the airline he had founded. Consequently, a firm relationship was established between CAS and

Announce that all their flights will operate from

BRISTOL (LULSGATE) AIRPORT

as from

SUNDAY 14th April, 1957

Coach transport to Bristol (Lulsgate) Airport will leave the City Centre as indicated below

BRISTOL TRAMWAYS OFFICE

70 minutes prior to aircraft departure time

TEMPLE MEADS RAILWAY STATION

65 minutes prior to aircraft departure time

The End. The card produced by Cambrian Airways in April 1957 to inform passengers of the transfer of services from Whitchurch to Lulsgate Bottom. (Author's Collection)

Postscript. On 10 November 1993, some 36 years after the airport closed, this Cessna 152 made an emergency landing at Whitchurch, low on fuel. Compare this photo with that of a B-17 Fortress in roughly the same position on 24 September 1943. Also see the photos on pages 125 and 126. (A Hartles)

BEA, and in 1953 the State airline acquired a share holding in what, in effect, had become the Welsh national airline. With the departure of S Kenneth Davies, Wing Commander L B 'Bill' Elwin AFC took over as Managing Director, with Mr B J T 'Jim' Callan as Operations Manager, and under their direction the company experienced steady growth.

In 1955 Cambrian Air Services was renamed Cambrian Airways, but that year the company suffered a fatal accident. This occurred on 23 July, when Dove G-AKSK crashed in the New Forest while operating the Cardiff–Paris (Le Bourget) service, with intermediate stops at Bristol and Southampton. The first part of the flight progressed normally, but approaching Southampton engine problems resulted in the aircraft crashing at Fritham. Sadly, Capt R J 'Bob' Carson was killed, but all six passengers on board survived. At the time of this accident the other pilots regularly flying Rapides and Doves through Whitchurch with Cambrian were Captains G A Perrott (Chief Pilot), A Townsend, R C de Wilde, T Thomas, G E Keeble, P E Hendy, J A Gibson, K G Wakefield and L G Roberts.

Over the next three years Cambrian achieved an annual traffic growth of around 15 per cent and by 1957, when Whitchurch closed, it was providing services to Jersey, Guernsey, Dinard, Cardiff, Southampton, Paris, London, Manchester, Glasgow, Belfast, Cheltenham and Gloucester (Staverton) and Nice. Before long the airline was to become a wholly owned subsidiary of BEA, which itself was destined to merge with BOAC to become the British Airways of today, but Cambrian was still operating under its own name when Whitchurch closed. By this time it was the principal airline serving the West Country and Wales and it retained this position after moving to Bristol's new airport at Lulsgate. Interestingly, in 1959 a re-organised Cambrian Airways standardised its equipment on Dakotas supplied by BEA, and among them were three – G-AGHM, G-AGHS and G-AGIP – that had been with BOAC at Whitchurch during the war. Their return to the Bristol area was short-lived, however, for by 1962 Cambrian was phasing out its faithful Dakotas in favour of more modern equipment. Expansion continued and by the early Seventies the airline was operating 19 Viscounts and four BAC One-Elevens on a much expanded domestic and international route network, but in 1976, by which time Cambrian had lost its separate identity within a newly formed BA Regional Division, its operations from Bristol ceased. Dan-Air, which had been operating a Bristol–Cardiff–Liverpool service for some time, and other independent airlines then took over some of the services previously operated by Cambrian/British Airways.

Following the closure of Whitchurch in the Spring of 1957, much of the old grass landing area was made available for sports purposes. In due course some of the buildings on the South Side, including the Club House, were demolished but others were erected in their place for commercial or industrial purposes. One building was used as a book depos-

A B-17 Fortress, Fairchild Argus and Avro Anson at Whitchurch on 24 September 1943. Compare with previous photo. (M Olmsted via A Hartles)

itory, while others went to a road haulage contractor and John Harvey and Sons, Ltd., the long established Bristol firm of sherry producers, who set up a large depot on the site. Still in residence at Whitchurch (as had been the case since 1940), the Bristol Aeroplane Company continued to overhaul engines for both civil and military aircraft. Much of this work was now carried out on the North Side, where the Company had taken over some of the buildings occupied until 1952 by the BOAC Stores Depot, but it also retained some of its South Side premises. Although mainly concerned with its own products – initially Hercules and Centaurus piston engines, followed by Proteus, Olympus and Orpheus gas turbines – the Company also carried out overhauls on engines manufactured by General Electric and Pratt and Whitney, but the end came in 1971, when it was decided to close the Whitchurch facility and transfer engine overhauls to Patchway.

Flying officially came to an end at Whitchurch on 13 April 1957. 'Officially' is a necessary qualification, however, because several aircraft, among them a Dakota of Dan-Air, landed there by mistake long after the airport had been closed and its Air Traffic Control and other services transferred to the new Bristol (Lulsgate) Airport. And as recently as November 1993 a Cessna 152 light aircraft inbound to Lulsgate made an emergency landing at Whitchurch with a fuel shortage problem.

During the 27 years of its operating existence – covering what many regard as the Golden Age of aviation – few aerodromes can have seen a greater variety of aircraft and air activity than Whitchurch. Indeed, its closing was more than just the end of an airport; it was the end of an era.

APPENDIX I

The Bristol & Wessex Aeroplane Club

AIRCRAFT OPERATED, 1929–1957

Regn	Type	Period in Service/Remarks
G-EBSN	de Havilland DH 60X Moth	26 July 1927 - 6 May 1928
G-EBKK	Parnall Pixie III	1927 - September 1930 (Donated by George Parnall & Co)
G-EBJL	Bristol 91A Brownie	5 Sept 1929 - 24 Nov 1932 (Donated by the Bristol Aeroplane Co)
G-EBTV	de Havilland DH 60X Moth	19 October 1927 - 1932
G-EBXF	de Havilland DH 60X Moth	23 May 1928 - 1932
G-EBYH	de Havilland DH 60X Moth	3 July 1928 - May 1931
G-AACD	de Havilland DH 60M Moth	November 1929 (On loan from DH Aircraft Co)
G-AASR	de Havilland DH 60M Moth	2 December 1929 - October 1934
G-ABKL	Spartan Arrow	4 April 1931 - October 1932
G-ABTP	de Havilland DH 60G Gipsy Moth	12 February 1932 - January 1936
G-ABWM	de Havilland DH 60G Gipsy Moth	20 May 1932 - January 1936
–	de Havilland DH 82 Tiger Moth	1932 (On loan from DH Aircraft Co)
G-ACPT	de Havilland DH 60GIII Moth Major	1 June 1934 - May 1936
G-ACXP	Cierva C.30A Autogiro	28 Sept 1934 - December 1934
G-ADFD	Avro 643 Cadet	24 May 1935 - 1 September 1939
G-AEAU	BA (Pobjoy) Swallow II	30 Jan 1937 - June 1939
G-AEAV	BA (Pobjoy) Swallow II	30 Feb 1936 - 1 Sept 1939
G-AESL	BA (Cirrus) Swallow II	20 Jan 1937 - 1 Sept 1939
G-AFAZ	Foster Wikner GM.1 Wicko	19 Sept 1938 - 1 Sept 1939
G-AEGN	BA Swallow II	April 1939 - 1 September 1939
G-AFOT	de Havilland DH 94 Moth Minor	7 July 1939 - 1 September 1939
G-AFOU	de Havilland DH 94 Moth Minor	29 July 1939 - 1 September 1939
G-AFOV	de Havilland DH 94 Moth Minor	26 Aug 1939 - 1 Sept 1939 (Not delivered)
G-AHWJ	Taylorcraft Plus Model D	7 August 1946 - September 1959
G-AHWK	Taylorcraft Plus Model D	25 October 1946 - September 1952
G-AHWI	Taylorcraft Plus Model D	7 February 1947 - October 1951
G-AGVM	Auster J/1 Autocrat	April 1948 - 19 May 1959
G-AHCN	Auster J/1 Autocrat	March 1949 - 1964
G-AMBK	de Havilland DH 82A Tiger Moth	16 June 1950 - July 1953
G-AJHU	de Havilland DH 92A Tiger Moth	25 July 1953 - April 1961
G-ANSM	de Havilland DH 82A Tiger Moth	August 1955 - July 1960

APPENDIX II

Norman Edgar and Western Airways, Ltd.

AIRCRAFT OPERATED, 1930–1939

Entered Service	Regn	Type
1931	G-AARA	de Havilland DH 60G Gipsy Moth
1932	G-ABYO	de Havilland DH 83 Fox Moth (Written off 16.6.34)
1932	G-ABWZ	de Havilland DH 80A Puss Moth
1932	G-ABFV	de Havilland DH 80A Puss Moth
1932	G-ABBS	de Havilland DH 80A Puss Moth
1933	G-ACJT	de Havilland DH 84 Dragon I (Written off 20.12.39)
1935	G-ACMP	de Havilland DH 84 Dragon II (Written off 22.7.35)
1935	G-ACAO	de Havilland DH 84 Dragon I
1936	G-ACMJ	de Havilland DH 84 Dragon I
1937	G-ADDD	de Havilland DH 89 Dragon Rapide
1937	G-ACTU	de Havilland DH 89 Dragon Rapide
1938	G-ACPX	de Havilland DH 84 Dragon II
1938	G-AECZ	de Havilland DH 84 Dragon II (Sold March 1939)
1938	G-ADBV	de Havilland DH 89 Dragon Rapide
1939	G-AEDH	de Havilland DH 90 Dragonfly
1939	G-AFIX	Percival P.16A Q.6
1939	G-AETM	de Havilland DH 86B Express
1939	G-AFSO	de Havilland DH 89A Dragon Rapide
1939	G-AFVC	Percival P.14A Q.6
1939	G-ACLE	de Havilland DH 84 Dragon I

APPENDIX III

No. 33 Elementary & Reserve Flying Training School

AIRCRAFT OPERATED, 1938–1939

Type	Serial No	Received
de Havilland DH 82A Tiger Moth II	N5472	3.12.38
de Havilland DH 82A Tiger Moth II	N5476	3.12.38
de Havilland DH 82A Tiger Moth II	N5478	3.12.38
de Havilland DH 82A Tiger Moth II	N5474	6.12.38
de Havilland DH 82A Tiger Moth II	N5475	6.12.38
de Havilland DH 82A Tiger Moth II	N5477	6.12.38
Hawker Hind (T)	K6805	29.11.38
Hawker Hind (T)	K5439	1.12.38
Hawker Audax	K3082	–
Hawker Audax	K3702	2.12.38
Hawker Hind	K5435	12.1.39
Hawker Hind	K5491	8.5.39
Avro Anson Mk I	N5306	8.8.39
Avro Anson Mk I	N5307	8.8.39

Note: *This is a list of known aircraft only and is not complete.*

APPENDIX IV

Imperial Airways & British Airways (National Air Communications)

AIRCRAFT BASED AT WHITCHURCH, SEPTEMBER 1939

Armstrong Whitworth AW 27 Ensign ('E' Class):

G-ADSR *Ensign*
G-ADSS *Egeria*
G-ADST *Elsinore*
G-ADSU *Euterpe*
G-ADSV *Explorer*
G-ADSW *Eddystone*
G-ADSX *Ettrick*
G-ADSY *Empyrean*
G-ADSZ *Elysian*

Note: Ensigns arriving at Whitchurch later (in 1940) were G-ADTA *Euryalus* G-ADTB *Echo* and G-ADTC *Endymion.*

de Havilland DH 91 Albatross ('F' Class):

G-AFDI *Frobisher*
G-AFDJ *Falcon*
G-AFDK *Fortuna*
G-AFDL *Fingal*
G-AFDM *Fiona*

Handley Page HP 42E & 42W:

G-AAUD *Hanno*
G-AAXC *Heracles*
G-AAXD *Horatius*

Junkers Ju 52/3m:

G-AERU *Juno*
G-AERX *Jupiter*
G-AFAP *Jason*

Note: All three aircraft departed Whitchurch for Perth in October 1939.

Lockheed lOA Electra:

G-AEPN G-AEPO G-AEPR G-AFCS G-AFEB

Lockheed 12A:

G-AEMZ G-AEOI

Lockheed 14-WF62:

G-AFGP G-AFGR G-AFKD G-AFKE G-AFMO G-AFMR G-AFYU

Short 5.17/L:

G-ACJJ *Scylla*
G-ACJK *Syrinx*

APPENDIX V

No. 2 Ferry Pool, Air Transport Auxiliary

TAXI AIRCRAFT BASED AT WHITCHURCH, 1940–1945

Airspeed Courier:

G-ACZL

Avro Anson:

N1339 N4875 N4877 N4917 N4971 N5060 N5110 N5154 N5256 N5295 N5381
N9543 N9546 N9552 N9567 N9657 N9674 N9782 N9785 N9825 N9827 N9930
N9934 N9955 N9972 N9977 R3329 R3375 R3429 R3459 R9586 R9667 R9719
R9753 W1732 W1792 W1827 AX352 AX375 AX501 AX504 AX544 AX558

EF939 EG228 EG292 EG374 EG379 EB442 LT729 LT827 LV137 MG219 MH132
NK492 NK544 NK774 NK784 NK822 NK864 NK808 NK824 NK872 NK905

Fairchild 24W-41 Argus:

EV751 EV771 EV772 EV775 EV766 EV777 EV779 EV780 EV785 EV790 EV791
EV794 EV795 EV796 EV803 EV805 EV807 EV809 EV811 FK314 FK315 FK334
FK335 FK338 FK343 FK344 FK347 FK348 FK359 FK361 HB574 HB592 HB596
HB559 HB599 HB603 HB624 HB630 HM164 HM165 HM168 HM169 HM170
HM172 HN176 HM183 HM184 HM186 HM188

Fairey Battle (T):

P6758

Piper J4 Cub Coupe:

BV988 (formerly G-AFVM)

Note: *This list shows aircraft known to have been on strength at various times between 1940 and 1945 and is not necessarily complete.*

APPENDIX VI

KLM Royal Dutch Airlines

AIRCRAFT BASED AT WHITCHURCH, JUNE 1940

Type	Regn	Previous Regn	Name
Douglas DC-2-115F	G-AGBH	PH-ALE	*Edelvalk*
Douglas DC-3-178	G-AGBB	PH-ALI	*Ibis*
Douglas DC-3-194B	G-AGBC	PH-ALR	*Reiger*
Douglas DC-3-194C	G-AGBD	PH-ARB	*Buizerd*
Douglas DC-3-194D	G-AGBE	PH-ARZ	*Zilverreiger*
Douglas DC-3-194D	G-AGBI	PH-ARW	*Wulp*

APPENDIX VII

No. 1 Line, BOAC

AIRCRAFT BASED AT WHITCHURCH, 31 MARCH 1945.

Type	Regn/Serial	Remarks (including RAF Serial Nos and Transport Command Code Markings).
Airspeed Oxford II	R6070	On loan from the RAF.
"	DF521	On loan from the RAF.
"	HN832	On loan from the RAF.
"	AP474	On loan from the RAF.
"	NM536	On loan from the RAF.
Douglas DC-2	G-AGBH	KLM aircraft on charter to BOAC.
Douglas DC-3	G-AGBD	KLM aircraft on charter to BOAC.
Douglas DC-3	G-AGBE	KLM aircraft on charter to BOAC.
Douglas C-47A Dakota III	G-AGHJ	FD867/ODZX
"	G-AGHM	FD901/ODZW
"	G-AGHN	FD868/ODZV
"	G-AGHO	FD941/ODZU
"	G-AGHP	FD862/ODZT
"	G-AGHR	FL514/ODZS
"	G-AGHS	FL516/ODZR
"	G-AGHT	FL520/OSZQ
"	G-AGHU	FD942/ODZP
"	G-AGIP	FL544/ODZO
"	G-AGIS	FL607/ODZM
"	G-AGIT	FL560/ODZN
"	G-AGIY	FZ567/ODZL
"	G-AGJR	KLM aircraft on charter to BOAC.
"	G-AGJS	KLM aircraft on charter to BOAC.
"	G-AGJT	KLM aircraft on charter to BOAC.
"	G-AGJU	FZ614/ODZG
"	G-AGJV	FZ638/ODZF
"	G-AGJW	FZ641/ODZD
"	G-AGJX	FL604/ODZC
"	G-AGJY	FL608/OSZB
"	G-AGJZ	FL629/ODZA
Douglas C-47B Dakota IV	G-AGKB	KJ804/OFZX
"	G-AGKC	KJ807/OFZW
"	G-AGKD	KJ811/OFZV
"	G-AGKE	KJ867/OFZU
"	G-AGKG	KJ879/OFZS

"	G-AGKH	KJ871/OFZR
"	G-AGKI	KJ928/OFZQ
"	G-AGKJ	KJ933/OFZP
"	G-AGKK	KJ929/OFZO
"	G-AGKL	KJ935/OFZN
"	G-AGKM	KJ992/OFZM
"	G-AGKN	KJ990/OFZL
"	G-AGMZ	KJ985/OFZK
"	G-AGND	KK142/OFZF
"	G-AGNE	KK139/OFZD
"	G-AGNF	KK201/OFZC
"	G-AGNG	KK216/OFZB
"	G-AGNK	KK206/OFZA

APPENDIX VIII

Airways Aero Club

AIRCRAFT BASED AT WHITCHURCH, 1949–1952

Aeronca 100	G-AEXD	
de Havilland DH 80A Puss Moth	G-AEOA	
de Havilland DH 82A Tiger Moth	G-ALOX	(On temporary loan from AAC, Hurn)
Miles M.14A Hawk Trainer III	G-AFBS	(Initially registered G-AKKU in error)
Miles M.14A Hawk Trainer III	G-AKKR	
Miles M.14A Hawk Trainer III	G-AKKZ	
Percival Proctor 3	G-ALSM	(Owned by L W Watkins, on loan to AAC)
Piper J3 Cub	G-AFFJ	(Owned by E V Pyle, on loan to AAC)
Taylorcraft Auster Mk V	G-AJVU	(Owned by J Shuckburgh, on loan to AAC)

APPENDIX IX

Cambrian Air Services/ Cambrian Airways

AIRCRAFT OPERATING FROM WHITCHURCH, 1953–1957

Aircraft	Registration	Notes
Auster J/1 Autocrat	G-AGYT	Used for positioning crews between Cardiff and Bristol. Sold in 1956.
de Havilland DH 104 Dove IB	G-AIWF	Sold in 1957.
de Havilland DH 89A Rapide	G-AJCL *Flint*	To BEA in 1959, for Lands End-Scillies service.
de Havilland DH 104 Dove IB	G-AJOT	Sold in 1956.
de Havilland DH 104 Dove IB	G-AKSK	Crashed in the New Forest, 23 July 1955.
de Havilland DH 104 Dove IB	G-AKSS	On lease from Independent Air Transport, 1956.
de Havilland DH 89A Rapide	G-AKUB *Glamorgan*	Sold in 1955.
de Havilland DH 89A Rapide	G-AKUC *Monmouth*	Sold in 1955.
de Havilland DH 89A Rapide	G-ALAT *Anglesey*	Sold in 1954.
de Havilland DH 89A Rapide	G-ALZJ *Caernarvon*	Sold in 1956.
Douglas C-47B Dakota IV	G-AMSW	In use from 1954.
Douglas C-47B Dakota IV	G-AMSX	In use from 1955.
de Havilland DH 114 Heron 1B	G-ANCI	On lease from Overseas Air Transport, 1957.
de Havilland DH 114 Heron 2	G-AOGO	In use from 22 March 1956.
de Havilland DH 114 Heron 2	G-AOGU	In use from 27 March 1956.
de Havilland DH 114 Heron 2E	G-AORJ	In use from 22 June 1956.

Index

For ease of reference the Index is divided into three sections - General, People and Aircraft. References to Bristol and Whitchurch Airport have been omitted because of the frequency with which these place names appear in the text.

General

PEOPLE

Aircraft